Praise for ***Engendering Cosmopolitanism Through the Local***

"*Engendering Cosmopolitanism Through the Local* by Jacquelyn Chappel is a timely book that engages with the complexities of cosmopolitanizing the teaching of literature through the use of international literature. The book usefully distinguishes between multicultural and global education as well as world literature and international literature while acknowledging the overlaps among these terms. A key strength of the book is the examples of cosmopolitanism-on-the-ground through rich and nuanced examples of the ways teachers attempt to introduce international literature and the challenges that occur as teachers attempted to connect foreign culture with students' lived experiences. The book provides an original and important contribution to the ever-growing field of cosmopolitan studies in English education."

Suzanne Choo, Assistant Dean and Assistant Professor,
National Institute of Education, Nanyang Technological University

"This book invites teachers to engage with the potentials of cosmopolitanism for transforming their teaching of World Literature by providing practical examples of how these theories play out in secondary classrooms. These classroom examples demonstrate how supporting students in critically connecting to their own cultural values provides a context within which they can become more critically open to values that differ from their own—connecting the local with the global. This book challenges educators to move beyond the Euro-centered approaches that continue to dominate World Literature, despite good intentions, and instead engage readers in critical dialogue about international literature."

Kathy Short, Professor, University of Arizona; Director, Worlds of Words

Engendering Cosmopolitanism Through the Local

This book is part of the Peter Lang Education list.
Every volume is peer reviewed and meets
the highest quality standards for content and production.

PETER LANG
New York • Bern • Berlin
Brussels • Vienna • Oxford • Warsaw

Jacquelyn Chappel

Engendering Cosmopolitanism Through the Local

Engaging Students in International Literature Through Connections to Personal Experience and Culture

PETER LANG
New York • Bern • Berlin
Brussels • Vienna • Oxford • Warsaw

Library of Congress Cataloging-in-Publication Data

Names: Chappel, Jacquelyn, author.
Title: Engendering cosmopolitanism through the local: engaging students in international literature through connections to personal experience and culture / Jacquelyn Chappel.
Description: New York: Peter Lang, 2019.
Includes bibliographical references and index.
Identifiers: LCCN 2018057309 | ISBN 978-1-4331-6416-3 (hardback: alk. paper)
ISBN 978-1-4331-6415-6 (paperback: alk. paper) | ISBN 978-1-4331-6014-1 (ebook pdf)
ISBN 978-1-4331-6015-8 (epub) | ISBN 978-1-4331-6016-5 (mobi)
Subjects: LCSH: Literature—Study and teaching.
Cosmopolitanism in literature. | Multicultural education.
Classification: LCC PN56.C683 C53 2019 | DDC 809/.933552—dc23
LC record available at https://lccn.loc.gov/2018057309
DOI 10.3726/b14960

Bibliographic information published by **Die Deutsche Nationalbibliothek**.
Die Deutsche Nationalbibliothek lists this publication in the "Deutsche Nationalbibliografie"; detailed bibliographic data are available on the Internet at http://dnb.d-nb.de/.

Table of Contents

Figures and Tables

Figure

Tables

Acknowledgments

I would like to thank Margaret Maaka for taking me on as an advisee; Hannah Tavares for providing feedback on early chapters; Patricia Halagao for her enthusiasm; Todd Sammons for his long-standing and multifaceted support; Charlotte Frambaugh-Kritzer for her steadfast support; Julie Kaomea for her sage counsel and advice; Phan Le Ha for pushing me to write and publish; Subramanian Shankar for indulging my questions; Britton Brooks, Jade Higa, and Laura Wang for providing early feedback and encouragement, particularly to Laura Wang for bringing Amy Tan's memoir to my attention; Mary Chang who encouraged the completion of this book project; Suzanne Choo for providing counsel as my research questions were first percolating; Sarah Twomey for her early support and for facilitating the professional development opportunities that led to the development of the curriculum in this book; Yun Peng whose expertise and insights made much of this book possible; Rich Milner for his encouragement to publish *immediately*; Erin Kahunawai Wright for her encouragement and practical insights; Rodney Morales for his insights on local literature in Hawai'i; Bill Teter and Monica Ka'imipono for sharing their teacher journeys; the

English Department at the University of Hawai'i, whose coursework and department culture planted the seeds for exploration on issues of authenticity and representation; all the teachers who shared with me their experiences of teaching "World Literature"; and the peer reviewers and editors, Sarah Bode and Megan Madden, who recognized the value of this project. Thank you.

Chapter One

Introduction

Today, many educators regard multicultural education as a positive, worthwhile, and even benign goal. Multicultural education, which James Banks defined as pedagogy designed to "reform schools and other education institutions … so that students from diverse racial, ethnic, and social-class groups will experience educational equality" (Banks, 1993) is aimed at broadening school curriculum to include the voices and histories of marginalized individuals. Multicultural education began with an interest in sharing those stories which had been rendered invisible. Multicultural curriculum, often regarded as a means to promote tolerance and open mindedness among our students, aligns with many of the goals of education itself—which seeks to create ethically-minded, civicly-engaged individuals. Despite these seemingly innocuous goal, multicultural education has been critiqued on many fronts.

In the 1990s, conservatives such as E. D. Hirsch (1988) and Alan Bloom (1987) critiqued multicultural education for contributing to the dissolution of a common cultural heritage and national identity. While defenders of multiculturalism pointed out the need to include the voices of ethnic minorities long absent from formal school curricula, traditionalists defended the importance of a shared national heritage and the need for schools to impart cultural literacy.

Liberals too have critiqued multicultural education for its overemphasis on superficial differences such as holidays and tradition. Some pointed out that in practice multicultural education often devolves into lessons on food, clothing, and holidays that do not necessarily promote tolerance or understanding. This "three F's approach … to food, folk/festivals and fun" exoticizes difference and avoids engagement with structural inequalities in schools and in society (Richardson, 2011, p. 108). "[L]ook[ing] at culture through [these] categories actually reinforce[s] stereotypes and mainstream domination," Fox and Short point out (2003, p. 22).

Multicultural education has been critiqued for its narrow definition which often applies only to marginalized ethnicities. Excluding the stories and experiences of marginalized genders (Pang, 2001; Sleeter & Grant, 1999), multicultural education focuses too heavily on race, ethnicity, and class and overlooks the experiences of gay, transgender, and queer individuals as well as the disabled, whose stories are acutely important to the young people navigating these identities and experiences (Loutzenheiser, 1996; Loutzenheiser & MacIntosh, 2004).

Outside of education, multiculturalism has been critiqued for emphasizing and thereby reifying racial and ethnic differences that are oftentimes meaningless. Keenan Malik describes the policies surrounding multiculturalism as institutionalizing diversity by putting people into ethnic and cultural boxes when our racial, ethnic, and cultural categories are not so easily defined. Rather than ameliorating racial and ethnic strife, multiculturalism has contributed to further tension, he maintains (Malik, 2013). Multiculturalism has done more harm than good.

So heavily critiqued is multicultural education, the term has fallen out of favor. In lieu of "multicultural education," the buzz word in education today is "diversity," a similarly vague and loaded term with many of the same pitfalls of multicultural education.

Watching the Olympics but Only Your Country

This book presents yet another critique of multicultural education, which since the 1990s to today—particularly in the United States—has tended to focus on diversity within the nation at the expense of a truly global and international curriculum. Like spectators watching the Olympics but only watching their own country compete, students are engaging with diverse cultures but only with the cultures in their own nation. Rather than being exposed to the viewpoints of a country other than their own, students are exposed to multicultural lessons essentially about their own country. As a result, Americans understand Vietnam only through the prism of the Vietnam War—one part of the country's long history. For others, the wider world is understood only through the immigrants and refugees in their country's borders.

The importance of the distinction between multicultural and global education are well-noted. Father of multicultural education James Banks himself noted their overlapping purposes and the importance of the distinction. In making the case for multicultural education, he pointed out how many confused the goals of multicultural and global education, because both share the purpose of cross-cultural competency (Banks, 1994). Banks, however, noted, "Although the goals of multicultural education are complimentary [to global studies], they need to be distinguished both conceptually and in practice" (p. 18). The frequent conflation of multicultural and global education has been observed in passing (Banks, 1994; Cai, 2003a; Choo, 2013; Loh, 2009; Spivak, 2003) but never in much depth.

To be clear, K–12 Language arts practitioners and scholars have gone to great lengths to define their terms. According to the prevailing scholarship, multicultural literature refers to literature featuring diverse cultures *set in the reader's country* while global literature refers to stories *set outside the reader's home country* (Lehman, Freeman, & Scharer, 2010). According to this definition, global literature can be written by authors with a wide variety of backgrounds including: authors not descended from the countries they write about, generally considered "outsiders" to the culture they write about; authors drawing on their family's cultures but who may have never visited these countries themselves; immigrants from a country, generally considered "insiders" to that culture (Short, Evans, & Hilebrand, 2011, p. 34); international authors such as Chinua Achebe publishing outside their home country; and finally international authors, originally publishing, translated or untranslated, in the country they write about (Lehman et al., 2010).

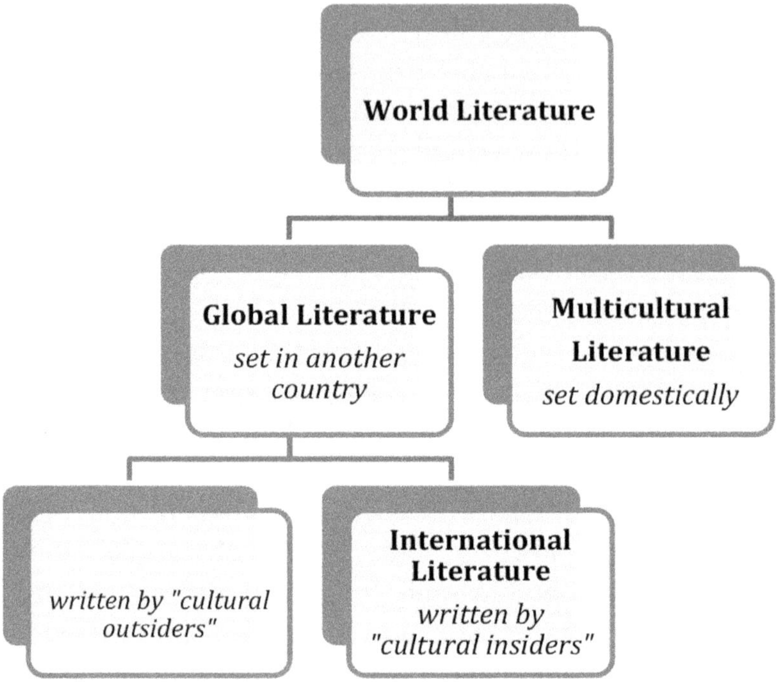

Figure 1.1: World, Global and International Literature in K–12 Curriculum.
Source: Author.

This book takes particular interest in the final two categories, which I refer to as *international literature,* literature written by "cultural insiders." Generally regarded as individuals claiming provenance to a certain nation or region as a result of cultural or linguistic identification with a nation, cultural insiders are often, but not always, defined by citizenship.

These myriad distinctions are important, because they inform the potentially explosive issues of authenticity and representation latent when reading cross culturally. In Hawai'i, for example, where the teacher stories in this book are situated, the literature of Hawai'i and the Pacific was long defined by sojourners through Hawai'i such as Jack London, Robert Louis Stevenson, and Herman Melville. This problematic practice, which perpetuated wrongs both aesthetically and politically (Chappel, 2017), confirmed colonial attitudes about Hawai'i and suggested that the people of Hawai'i and the Pacific had no literary tradition of their own. Who writes about the cultures being represented matters. These representations are important for the people being represented and should be important for the readers attempting to grasp those cultures.

The distinctions of author provenance have been handled diffently in World Literature, a course of study offered in the secondary and post-secondary levels particularly in the United States and in Britain (Lawall, 2009; Pizer, 2006) that purports to capture all of the great literature of the world (Cai, 2003a; Cheah, 2014; Damrosch, 2003). While World Literature is sometimes perceived as synonymous with international literature, World Literature has historically featured mainly English language texts from Britain and the United States. At the secondary level, it often features Westerners writing about non-Western cultures. It has featured the writings of immigrants writing about their immigrant experience. And it has featured the writings of ethnic minorities representing their heritage countries. In short, as an umbrella term including all the literatures of the world, World Literature has included both multicultural and global literature. These practices are problematic particularly when reading lists attempt to categorize texts by nation.

In an attempt to engage their students, multicultural educators have employed literature by ethnic minorities in introducing the stories and experiences of other parts of the world. "It is through the literature of ethnicity that we customarily approach the question of globality," Spivak observed (2003, pp. 82–83). Since ethnicity has long been tied to nationality, she points out, it makes sense that educators might equate racial/ethnic make-up with one's country of origin.

Using multiculturalism as a means to engage students with international contexts leverages content relevant to students' lives while making connections outside of their home country. For example, some World Literature teachers have argued this is vitally important particularly for the displaced students in their classroom. In Spencer's classrooms in Britain, she saw that her Asian Indian and Caribbean students needed to read literature from their home countries in order to see that "their stories, their traditions, had value" (Spencer, 1994, p. 335). While this curriculum connected students to experiences and histories relevant to them, numerous scholars since Spencer have pointed out the landmines that can emerge in singling students out based on their ethnic background (Dudley-Marling, 2003; Gaudelli, 2003). Spencer also stops short of describing which texts and specific pedagogical strategies she employed.

In others teachers' World Literature course, lessons on "border crossings" between the United States and Mexico, for example, helped engage students with cultures in their backyard. In her World Literature course, multicultural literature helped students access a culture and immigration history that were relevant to her students (Downing, 2002) and therefore more likely to engage them. Still, teachers employed texts by American authors even while calling for an "authentic World Literature curriculum" (Kerschner, 2002, p. 78), raising the question of both cultural authenticity and the definition of World Literature.

More egregious, websites of popular World Literature reading lists have conflated national and ethnic identity, demonstrating confusion between the two. While the reading list denotes texts by country—for example "China," "India," and "Cambodia"—when identifying the countries of ethnic American authors Gary Soto and Rudolfo Anaya, the website reverts to the moniker "Hispanic American." Canadian author Joy Kogawa is representative of "Japanese/Canada." And best-selling American author Amy Tan is representative of "China" (Top 100 World Literature Titles, 2018). These identifiers demonstrate how ethnic minority authors have been used as representative of international multiculturalism to the disservice of both ethnic American authors and the legitimate national literary traditions of many countries.

Increasingly many contemporary authors claim multiple nationalities. Accordingly, anthologies of World Literature have given up on categorizing authors and texts by national origin. Rather, some high school textbooks call the twentieth-century "A World Without Borders" (Beers, 2006). Longman's anthology of World Literature similarly drops national identifiers altogether (Puchner, 2012). Several theorists have argued that categorizing texts by time rather than national boundaries is appropriate in an age defined by global mobility and extraterritoriality (Cheah, 2014; Choo, 2013; Spivak, 2003). According to this approach, "citizenship is tied to the cosmos rather than the material world or state" and emphasizes common humanity across cultures (Choo, 2013, p. 131).

This laudable goal, however, ignores the real power differentials between countries. For example, in imagining a cosmopolitan approach to literature, Choo examines Mary Shelley's *Frankenstein* as an entry point to engage students with philosophical and religious questions. The cosmopolitan approach she offers promotes critical literacy while transcending cultural differences, she maintains. The popular text she offers as an example, however, is conspicuously a text of the British literary tradition published in the early 19th-century during a time of Britain's hegemonic dominance over the world. A classic of the British Romantic period, the text cannot help but represent a specific historical context and tradition and to reify beliefs about whose texts are worthwhile.

Choo's vision of a cosmopolitan literature looks forward to a time when authors' national and ethnic origins are immaterial. Based on the many post-colonial writers who maintain multiple national allegiances and write across national boundaries, we are already there; the Norton anthology's lack of national identifiers in its anthology of 20th-century literature illustrates that complexity of author identity and nationality and makes the point that national identifiers are often moot. It illustrates the very real possibility of a planetary and temporal approach to literature.

While literatures of the diaspora complicate issues of author identity, many nations including India, China, Britain, France, Nigeria and others do claim national literary traditions complete with their own periods, styles, and celebrated authors. An unwillingness to engage with these stories and styles in the context of their unique histories "reinforces Western modes of consumption and interpretation" (Venuti as cited in Nandi, 2013, p. 87) and contributes to a societal unwillingness to change for "*real* Others" [original emphasis] (as cited in Nandi, p. 88). What should educators who wish to introduce their students to a truly international literature do?

While an individual's nationality can change and individuals can maintain citizenship to multiple countries, our nationalities nevertheless impact our identities. A "citizenship based on the cosmos" overlooks the fact that extra-territorial entities are the exception rather than rule. In practice, our national identities influence the languages we are immersed in, the media we have access to, the laws we are subject to, our ability or inability to travel, our educational policies, and more. For these reasons, I hesitate to disregard the importance of nationality in author identity.

Rather, I would like to point out that including immigrant stories in a course premised on national differences highlights these authors' foreign status and further otherizes an already marginalized group. While the practice of including immigrant stories as World Literature might seem innocuous, it is not without its harms. Andrea Smith points out the political implications of perceiving ethnic Americans as perpetual foreigners, ineligible for citizenship. "It does not matter how long immigrants of color reside in the United States," she writes, "they will always be imaged as permanent foreign threats to empire." This logic, she points out, is most evident in anti-immigration movements particularly during wartime (Smith, 2006, p. 68). Recent immigrants to America, particularly Asian-Americans and Latino/a-Americans, have had a long history of being perceived as foreigners and the practice of reading ethnic Americans as proxies for international texts perpetuates this understanding of minorities as foreigners.

Chinese-American author Amy Tan agrees; representing a distinctly American point of view, Tan's texts belong in an American canon, she maintains.

> If I had to give myself any sort of label, I would have to say that I am an American writer. I am Chinese by racial heritage. I am Chinese-American by family and social upbringing. But I believe that what I write is American fiction by virtue of the fact that I live in this country and my emotional sensibilities, assumptions, and obsessions are largely American. My characters may be largely Chinese-American, but I think Chinese-Americans are part of America. (2003, p. 310)

A story about three generations of Chinese Americans in the US, written in English, published by an American publisher by an author born and raised in California, *The Joy Luck Club* is not a book of the Chinese literary canon but read and beloved by an American audience. While including these ethnic American selections in World Literature curriculum do indeed give voice to minorities, the placement of ethnic American texts as representative of their heritage country, unwittingly contribute to racist portrayals of ethnic Americans as outsiders in their home country.

In her survey of Asian American representations in literature, Elaine Kim notes that even American-born Asians who spoke English and had never visited their parents' country, were routinely asked when they had come from Asia, and when they were going back. These Asian Americans internalized the feeling that "English and the culture it reflected did not belong to them, and that they should pay attention to their 'Asian' roots" (Kim, 1976, p. 1). While some World Literature reading lists laudably give space to authentic Asian American voices, positioning them as World Literature, which includes foreign literature, highlights these ethnic Americans' outsider status. Just as narratives of "welcoming" and "belonging," and the careful usage of "us" and "them" in educational policy indicate the limits of belonging (Bryan, 2009) and indicate "new configurations" of racism (Garner, 2004 as cited in Bryan, 2009), highlighting "border crossings" and minority's immigrant experiences in a literature that presumes to be about foreign literature can result in exclusion rather than inclusion.

This book begins with the premise that we do a disservice by imparting lessons in international culture and history through multicultural education. Relying on multicultural literature in teaching World Literature contributes to two wrongs: 1. It perpetuates stereotypes of ethnic minorities as foreigners. 2. It misrepresents the legitimate literary traditions of many countries. In contrast to the cross-cultural issues that inevitably emerge in reading a translated text, in reading ethnic minority literature as representative of international literature, there is no border crossing. Such curriculum perpetuates insularity even as it claims to promote global coverage. Learning about international literature and culture through multicultural texts is like watching the Olympics but only watching for our own country's athletes. It amounts to a national self-centeredness that assumes our students are incapable of taking an interest in experiences outside their national experience.

While recognizing the dangers of using multicultural education as a proxy for lessons in international history and culture, this book also acknowledges that students learn best when teachers connect content to existing knowledge. This book attempts to reconcile the interest in creating a more cosmopolitan curriculum while speaking to the interests of the students in our regionally specific classrooms.

This book shares the challenges and successes of three high school teachers who engaged their students with literature outside their national experience. I first offer some background on World Literature, a term that has been used for a hundred years to refer to an international and transnational literary tradition. Next, I review the numerous well-documented challenges of teaching international literature. Finally, I offer some background on cosmopolitanism, a two thousand-year old concept referring to our ability to appreciate cultures and nations different from our own.

The experiences of the teachers highlighted here demonstrate that we can engage our students with international literature by connecting international texts topically or thematically with students' lived experiences. While the idea of drawing upon students' existing knowledge to promote learning is not novel (Moll, 1994), the idea that we can engender cosmopolitanism by leveraging students' local identities and experiences is counter-intuitive and seemingly oxymoronic. These teachers' experiences demonstrate that, even when teaching international literature, students learn best when teachers connect curriculum with prior knowledge. This book urges teachers to connect international literature to students' identities and experiences, not by relying upon multicultural literature, but by connecting the content to students' lives. The teachers here did so by leveraging students' ethnic identities, religious affiliations, and personal experiences.

Positionality/Setting

My interest in international education arose during my years teaching a high school course called World Literature over seven years between 2004–2012, a time of growing awareness of globalization. Thomas Friedman's *The World is Flat* (2005) urged everyone to recognize that the west had increasingly less of a competitive advantage over the rest of the world. Meanwhile, Tony Wagner's *The Global Achievement Gap* (2008), published in the wake of the global interest in country's Programme for International Student Assessment (PISA) scores, trumpeted the need for American education to be more competitive globally. Together with the explosion of social networking sites where my students were increasingly spending much of their lives, these texts suggested the narrative of an ever-shrinking world in which students were sure to interact with the rest of the world economically and socially. My interest in teaching international literature was therefore to introduce students to literature from the world, which I believed would be relevant to their lives.

As an English teacher in the United States for over a decade, I approach the issue of multicultural and international education from an American point of view and am guilty of the American insularity, which I critique. Like many English teachers (Monseau, 2002), I am familiar mainly with the English language American and British texts, which dominate World Literature, and my interest in World Literature arose largely out of the challenges I experienced in internationalizing my curriculum.

Although my curriculum is informed by American educational discourse, my research and the curriculum of the teachers featured here are situated in Hawai'i, a unique locality where place-based and culturally relevant curriculum have long been important. With linguistic, cultural, and historic ties to Tahiti and New Zealand, a plantation history which resulted in numerous immigrant groups from Asia and Europe settling in Hawai'i, and a colonial history which resulted in Hawai'i's eventually becoming a state of the US, Hawai'i is home to a distinct culture and demographic, not reflected in national textbooks or popular reading lists.

Given Hawai'i's unique culture and history, many teachers in Hawai'i have found it important to engage students to their particular lived experience in Hawai'i. And this was certainly true of the teachers featured in this book. Given the heightened need among many teachers to connect curriculum to the lives of students, Hawai'i presents a context where engaging students in international literature might prove doubly difficult. Although situated between Asia and the Americas, Hawai'i is nevertheless far removed from the events in both these places. It is the context of this unique and isolated island state that I ask: How do we keep our students from becoming parochial?

I would argue that an interest in one's local culture, demographic, and specific colonial history are not unique to Hawai'i. Teachers from Lubbock, Texas to Singapore to Bolivia face students immersed in their own distinct places and outlooks with their own set of colonial circumstances. How do we balance the parochial instincts of our students to engage with international literature?

A Brief History of World Literature

World Literature, a course of study that has attempted to broaden and internationalize literature curriculum for a hundred years, has had a tortuous history, which informs the various definitions of World Literature that circulate today. I offer a brief history here.

The term World Literature is attributed to Johann Wolfgang von Goethe who coined the term *weltliteratur* when he observed writers like Franz Kafka who succeeded in finding an audience outside of their home country. In 1827, Goethe famously remarked that "the epoch of world literature is at hand" (as cited in Damrosch, 2003). As a result of changes in communication and technology (Choo, 2013), these World Literature texts crossed national boundaries and, despite barriers in culture and even language, were widely read outside the author's home country, signaling a new global age in literature (Damrosch, 2003).

Despite the term's European origins, some contend that World Literature has been a uniquely American course of study (Lawall, 1994; Pizer, 2006), arising after World War I (Choo, 2014). The Lincoln High School curriculum, the first recorded curriculum involving World Literature in the United States, hoped to introduce students to texts outside the national traditions of British literature—which dominated literature curriculum, and American literature, then nascent (Choo, 2014). The study of literature from other parts of the world, it was hoped, would produce "world citizens with a sense of common humanity." The purpose of World Literature was then, as it is now, "to broaden reader's horizons through the encounter with cultural difference" (Damrosch, 2003, p. 121). Comparativists in the postwar era hoped World Literature would provide a cure for nationalism, separatism, jingoism and violence (Damrosch, 2003). Many looked to a course in World Literature as a "source of redemption from global trouble" (Smith, 2011, p. 585). "Wars and its aftermath motivated the urgent call for World Literature study," Smith writes (p. 591). In the aftermath of war with little-known, distant places becoming increasingly relevant to the United States, many hoped a course in World Literature would make American students into more global citizens with a better understanding of their place in the wider world. World Literature hoped to introduce students to foreign cultures to recognize their similarities and differences, a theme that recurs in World Literature pedagogy (Boglatz, 2005; Cooppan, 2009; Nandi, 2013; Needham, 2009; Reese, 2002; Richardson, 2011; Short, 2012; Thomas, 2007). Looking to the roots of the high school World Literature curriculum reminds educators that the interest in globalization in education is not new.

Even as some hoped World Literature would provide students a more global outlook, some anthologists designed World Literature curricula that sought to establish a cultural alliance between Europe and America and a "common Western heritage" (Nandi, 2013, p. 78). Richard Moulton's *World Literature and Its Place in General Culture* (1911) situates World Literature in the context of the English-speaking world. Philo Buck, the founder of Comparative Literature, similarly asserted a cultural alliance between Europe and America in contrast to non-western civilizations (Nandi, 2013). These courses, which emphasized the Anglo-European literary tradition, began to develop between the two world wars even as others hoped World Literature would be a "source of redemption from global trouble" (Smith, 2011).

Because of the daunting scope of World Literature, post-World War II interest in World Literature retracted into Comparative Literature, centered on a comparative study of the literatures of continental Europe (Spivak, 2009). Because no one could possibly know the entirety of world literatures, area studies experts, fluent in the languages of the source texts, retreated into their Comparative Literature departments, which tended to highlight the Romance languages. English departments remained true to their expertise in texts originally written in English, and the interest in a broader non-Western literature curriculum was not realized.

Beginning as early as the 1960s and continuing into the 1980s and 1990s, post-colonial theorists, such as Edward Said and Gayatri Spivak, called the academy on their continued Eurocentric interpretation of World Literature in the Culture Wars. Spivak called World Literature a misnomer for a collection of primarily European works, while Said saw World Literature as colored by an Anglophone post-colonial past mired by Eurocentric approaches (Smith, 2011). World Literature has been called "NATO Literature," and is similarly attacked as a "Greater West European Co-Prosperity sphere" (Damrosch & Spivak, 2011, p. 460). Both labels attack World Literature's historically Eurocentric focus.

Traditionalists like Alan Bloom and E. D. Hirsch fired back, defending the need for a canon in order to preserve a sense of a Western cultural heritage. According to Bloom and Hirsch, a common curriculum ensured American students shared a sense of cultural literacy and tradition, one of the purposes of education. Bloom's vision of a canon drew heavily from European and Americans traditions (Damrosch, 2009), excluding both minority American literature and literature from non-Western nations.

One scholar meekly defended the canon by saying, "All the great literature is not here; perhaps all that is here is not great. But these stories are representative of the places and times from which they sprang" (Magill, cited in Damrosch, 2003, p. 124). As early as the 1960s, others made pleas to either broaden World Literature or abandon it altogether (Damrosch, 2003). No one won the Culture Wars, and while the issues remained the same, the tenor of the debate changed after the terrorist attack on the World Trade Center on September 11, which spurred America's increased military involvement in the Middle East and exacerbated tensions with immigrants to the US.

After 9/11, Americans were once again reminded about "our remote and foreign others" (Smith, 2011, p. 600), and the debate shifted away from canon formation. Scholars argued for a need to revisit the ethics of teaching and reading the literature of the global other. In this post-9/11 world, scholars, fed up with the debates over the canon, recognized the impossibility of introducing their students to everything they deemed "important". After 9/11, scholars once again recognized the urgent need to introduce students to the literatures of foreign countries outside the European tradition, regardless of whether or not agreement could be reached on an adequate reading list or definition of World Literature.

Today at the high school level, World Literature has several different definitions, arising from this tangled history. In my conversations with teachers over the years, teachers sometimes assumed World Literature referred to the canon of all the great literature of the world, represented by texts such as Homer's *The Odyssey* and the plays of Shakespeare. At other times, teachers assumed World Literature referred to texts by ethnic minority authors such Amy Tan and Sherman Alexie. At other times, World Literature referred to international literature including ancient sacred texts such as the *Epic of Gilgamesh* and contemporary texts such as Marjane Sartrapi's *Persopolis*. At other times still, World Literature referred to all literature, making it so pluripotent, it is no longer useful. So problematic is the term, many have called for doing away with "World Literature" altogether (Damrosch, 2003; Lawall, 2009; Shankar, 2012; Spivak, 2003; wa Thiong'o, 2012).

I use the term World Literature to refer to the courses of study as the teachers defined them. For this reason, the definitions of World Literature varied per the definitions listed above. While my ultimate interest lay in international literature, World Literature, as a course that has historically aimed to do this, offered a means to investigate the challenges and successes associated with internationalizing curriculum.

The Challenges of Teaching World Literature

While Lawall commented as early as 1994 that a preoccupation with the canon has stifled discussion on pedagogy, recent scholarship on World Literature seems to have finally given up on the goal of a common curriculum and turned its attention to these pedagogical concerns. This "pedagogical turn" has moved away from the impossible and never-ending task of defining a corpus to focusing on the challenges of doing justice to the foreign texts read in the classroom. However, numerous challenges face teachers of World Literature.

Finding Good Translated Texts

One of the first obstacles teachers face is accessing quality translations of international texts. According to a study by the Cooperative Children's Book Center in 2015, only 1–2 percent of children's books in the United States are translated (Short, Day, & Schroeder, 2016). While translations from English into non-English languages proliferate, translations from English continue to outpace translations into English (Damrosch 2003; Qualifications and Curriculum Authority, 2006), a fact which reflects English language's dominance in the publishing marketplace. Some have pointed out that this dominance of English language texts ironically contributes to provincialism among English language readers (Qualifications and Curriculum Authority, 2006). Whatever the result, the publication of international literature, particularly in translation, constitutes one of the root problems making access to texts difficult if not impossible.

Scope

Ironically, while publishing has been cited as a root problem in teaching World Literature, the vast scope of international literature also makes such an area of study impossible to master. The authoritative Norton's anthology of World Literature includes six volumes each totaling over a thousand pages (Puchner, 2012). High school compendiums of World Literature too frequently run over a thousand pages (Applebee & Littell, 2006; Bowler et al., 1996).

Educators have noted the virtual impossibility of any human being gaining expertise in all the literatures of the world (Damrosch, 2009; Lawall, 2009; Shankar, 2013). Even if teaching programs were to attempt to arm future English teachers with a grounding in literature from other parts of the world, the full scope of World Literature is simply too great to be covered. How can classroom teachers be expected to be knowledgeable in the traditions of China, India, Japan, Vietnam, Thailand, the Middle East, Polynesia, Britain, America, continental Europe, etc. while also having a firm ground in pedagogy? No one knows the world (Shankar, 2014). David Damrosch himself contends, "Who can really know enough to do it well?" (2009, p. 284).

Teacher Training

Closely related to the issue of scope, teachers weaned on a diet of British and American literature often do not have the expertise to teach a truly global literature. The foreign nature of World Literature and ingrained stereotypes of foreign national cultures make even well intentioned students resistant to non-stereotypical images of foreign cultures.

English teachers trained in the American and British tradition often do not have a firm grounding in literature of other cultures (Damrosch, 2003, 2009; Foster, 2009; Lawall, 1994; Robertson, 1974). In the *English Journal*'s issue on World Literature, published shortly after 9/11, the editor herself noted candidly, "I studied mostly British and American literature along with perhaps a few works by writers from predominantly Western countries," apologizing for the reality of today's teachers (Monseau, 2002, p. 1). "Most faculty members are likely to be trained in the traditional western canon," Lawall found, "[and] they are understandably uncomfortable in speaking not only from a vantage point of lesser authority but also with less cultural knowledge" (Lawall, 1994, p. 39). "Everyone was a rookie," Kerschner freely admits of the World Literature teachers at her school (2002, p. 80). With a lack of exposure to foreign texts in their own education, teachers often do not have a thorough enough grounding in World Literature to teach it confidently.

One educator argues that this presents an opportunity for teachers to make their own curricula (Robertson, 1974). But scholars have noted the limitations of teachers learning along with their students, where instructors unfamiliar with their curricula have the potential to grossly misrepresent cultures and perpetuate stereotypes when they attempt to teach about unfamiliar cultures. In the classroom, Kaomea (2006) observed that teachers unfamiliar with Hawaiian culture unwittingly perpetuated colonial myths. Relying upon the textbooks, which perpetuated untruths about Hawaiian culture, instructors unfamiliar with the cultures reinforced existing stereotypes. Because the stereotypes were all that many of these teachers knew on the subject, the stereotypes were all that were handed down.

The scenario Kaomea describes is mirrored in other classrooms across the country, where instructors unfamiliar with minority cultures unwittingly perpetuate stereotypes. In one elementary school lesson on a children's book about China, the teacher asked, "Now, boys and girls, look at this picture. What kind of outfit does this man wear? Is it the same as ours?" (Fang, Fu, & Lamme, 2003, p. 291). The teacher attempted to activate the children's background knowledge about Chinese culture through their prior knowledge. As a result, students were allowed to voice stereotypes without expansion or clarification. However, students were not encouraged to take critical perspectives, and the teacher reinforced the children's misconceptions. In addition, there was no discussion about the theme of the story, or the values, traditions, or symbols of the Chinese culture; rather, the discussion supported students' cultural misunderstandings (Fang et al., 2003). Spivak agrees with the critique of "learning along with the student" and argues, "We must earn the right to be able to judge what the student brings to the class" (p. 465). It's not enough to charge uninformed teachers with educating students about cultures that neither is well informed about, she maintains. Teachers must earn the right to be the teacher through their knowledge.

Negotiating Cultural Differences

Educators have noted that both students and teachers reading texts from unfamiliar cultures routinely encounter issues with overcoming established stereotypes, even when the curriculum explicitly seeks to overcome bias and stereotype (Cai, 2003b; Crocco, 2005; Dudley-Marling, 2003; Kaomea, 2006; Loh, 2009). These studies have found that teachers unfamiliar with the cultures they taught unwittingly perpetuated cultural stereotypes (Fang, Fu, & Lamme, 2003; Kaomea, 2006). Some teachers and scholars have even admitted to the racist baggage they bring to reading foreign texts (Nikola-Lisa, 2003). Students sometimes had a hard time believing that the three-dimensional characters written by cultural insiders were authentic (Crocco, 2005; Sung & Meyer, 2011), as their readings were framed by existing stereotypes (Kim, 1976, 1982). Students meanwhile often believed they came to texts with no biases (Loh, 2009), and teachers and students tended to not read in a culturally reflexive manner (Dudley-Marling, 2003; Loh, 2009; Jordan

& Purves, 1993). These studies pointed out that bias can occur in the classroom through:

- text selection (Crocco, 2005; Kim, 1982)
- lesson content (Kaomea, 2006)
- pedagogical approaches (Fang et al., 2003)
- teacher comments (Dudley-Marling, 2003)
- student comments (Loh, 2009)

Together, these studies suggest that issues of bias and ingrained stereotypes among teachers and students and in curricula have hampered a good reading of World Literature.

Indeed, educators have found that when students read texts about another culture, they look to confirm their previous understandings. In one example of a lesson on World Literature, pre-service teachers in a Social Studies Education Master's program read *Shabanu*, a novel about a young Pakistan girl written by American writer Suzanne Fisher Staples. Because it was recommended on many educational websites, the teacher believed the book portrayed Muslims as three-dimensional characters but was surprised by the divergent responses from the students. Euro-American students in the class disliked the book, saying the central character was too strong-willed to fit their conception of a Muslim girl. Pakistanis in the class, however, argued it should not be used in the classroom because the people teaching the book would have insufficient information on the culture, and the book would add to negative portrayals of Muslims (Crocco, 2005). Students' perceptions of the book, in other words, depended upon their cultural backgrounds, even at the Master's level.

Many students meanwhile believe they come to the text without any preconceptions. In a lesson on Ji-li Jiang's *Red Scarf Girl*, a young adult novel about the Cultural Revolution in China, for example, one 15-year-old boy in New York state commented, "I don't think there's any other special way we read it. It is from another place. We're just reading it" (Loh, 2009). Idealistic well-intentioned young adults, faced with the challenge of simply reading a book, may not realize the preconceptions they harbor. Indeed, studies have lamented that students do not read in a culturally reflexive manner (Dressel, 2005; Jordan &

Purves, 1993). This belief that students do not come to the text with any cultural baggage presents yet another barrier to cross-cultural understanding when reading World Literature.

The truth for many is that even well-intentioned individuals unwittingly harbor racist stereotypes. Nikola-Lisa (2003), educator and author of multi-cultural texts, admitted the racism he brings to his texts and life. Having grown up white in the South, he prides himself on growing up alongside Chicanos and Blacks, but one day, while on a road trip, he blithely suggested, "Why don't we sing it this way: Eenie, meenie, miney, moe, catch a nigg … nigg … nigg …" (p. 48). "I have seen the enemy, and it is myself," Nikola-Lisa writes (p. 48), acknowledging the racist language and attitudes he carries. While Nikola-Lisa remains committed and interested in multiculturalism, he understands his own personal limitations in representing a culture accurately, a burden shared by all teachers of World Literature.

Foreign Tropes, Genres, Styles, Sense of Humor

Another challenge in teaching international literature is that the style and content are foreign. Students unfamiliar with the culture may not be able to relate to the peculiarities of the text or the main character. And the text may not speak to students' experiences (Short, 2016). In reading the events of a world different from their own, students of World Literature are asked to understand foreign styles and senses of humor. The stock characters are often unfamiliar to students. The settings will be foreign. Indeed, the very genres may be different.

Literature from other parts of the world, some have noted, were not *meant* to be read by a foreign audience (Allan, 2007). Students of World Literature then are eavesdroppers, listening in on a conversation that is not about them and, further, not meant for them. "The leaps are larger in world literature" (Bingen, 2002, p. 40); as a result, teachers face challenges in engaging students in World Literature.

The question of a text's foreignness comes into focus when the issue of translation arises. Studying literature in translation is widely regarded as an impediment to appreciating the original text (Rose, 1996; Venuti, 2009). Any culture's language is steeped in its history and values, with each word suggesting meanings that the receiving culture may very easily miss. Lost in translation, the nuances create a gulf between students and the texts they are meant to engage with. Even a good translation—that is, one that attempts to remain true to the meaning of the original and takes care to evoke the intended tone of the original—may fall flat due the linguistic difference. Kyung-sook Shin's popular Korean novel, *Please Look After Mom*, for example, has been translated into English with some success. However, translations of even common everyday items in the text highlight yawning cultural differences and problems with translation. The "simple salted-cabbage dish," "lunch of rice and scabbard fish stew," and "fermented-bean-paste stew," (Shin, 2011, p. 143), meant to evoke nostalgic memories of a mother, would leave American readers in disgust.

Narrow Definitions of Literature

Finally, narrow definitions of what counts as literature represent a final obstacle to internationalizing literature curriculum. In *Decolonizing the Mind* (1981), Nigerian author and literary theorist wa Thiong'o pointed out that strict, Western ideas of literature have contributed to the lack of respect for the cultural productions of non-Western cultures, which are sometimes transmitted orally. In his treatise, wa Thiong'o makes a case for the importance of oral tradition.

Echoing wa Thiong'o, Shankar, in his introduction to a symposium on World Literature held at the University of Hawai'i in 2013, critiqued the tendency to study literature in isolation and to privilege the written text above oral tradition or folk literature. Speaking to an audience representing over a dozen nations from around the world, he made a plea to open up narrow understandings of literature in order to better capture the traditions of the world.

> [This] symposium poses questions on the very category of literature. It acknowledges that the notion of literature too should be complicated. The idea that literature should or could be studied in isolation from other cultural forms is a delusion. And perhaps worse, given that many cultures around the world find their most sustaining energy in the oral mode. In this context, the privileging of literature and indeed the very definition of it, that is, what

> counts as literature, appears doubly problematic. Not only is it critically tenable, but it also contributes to a predictable and ultimately violent hierarching of cultures. The symposium could be seen then to pose questions about the erasure of oratures within cultural theory in a symptomatic way as an illustration of other kinds of erasure under the problems attending the privileging of literature.

Western literary tradition, and by extension, World Literature, has systematically excluded and engaged in the erasure of valuable cultural practices, including folk and oral tradition, Shankar points out. The privileging of the written text over oral tradition has led to the dismissal of oral traditions as illegitimate forms of culture. For example, the emphasis on the written text as the only form of legitimate literature have led some to conclude that some Pacific Island cultures have no culture worthy of study, when in fact richly metaphoric Polynesian dance and song have been found to pass down actual geological histories (Dunn, 2001). In order to do justice to the "words of the world," Shankar suggests opening up the definition of literature and of text. Doing so has the potential to unearth a richer and more realistic vision of cultural traditions and texts that more accurately reflects the literatures of the world.

Many thinkers prior to Shankar and wa Thiong'o have made a similar observation: in his treatise *What is Literature*, Jean-Paul Sartre argued that the Western understanding of literature is an ideological construction (1965). Commenting on the same issues of the day, Foucault (1969) asserted that literature is understood differently in different places. In his philosophical investigation of the author, Foucault found that the way in which societies circulate, honor, attribute, and appropriate texts vary by culture. The importance of the author and the manner of distribution, in other words, vary from culture to culture depending on the populace's relationship to literature; definitions of literature will vary from place to place. In fact, author identity became important only after texts became transgressive and the individuals who wrote them needed to be punished. Together these authors point out that ideas of the author and of literature are constructed within unique cultures and histories. In keeping with this broader definition of literature to include various kinds of texts, World Literature might include not only the *Bhagavad Gita* but also the films of Bollywood, not only Zen parables but Japanese manga.

Given the numerous challenges facing educators in accessing texts, engaging students, and negotiating cultural differences, it is no wonder World Literature reading lists tend to recycle tried and true texts English language texts of Britain and the US. How can teachers overcome these obstacles to engage their students with international literature?

Cosmopolitanism and the Local

Cosmopolitanism, the philosophy suggesting a world citizenship, offers a theory that might help to understand how to engage students with international literature. Often traced back to the Roman Stoics and Enlightenment philosophers, cosmopolitanism proposes cultivating a sense of shared humanity. Literally translated as "kosmou polites" or "citizen of the world," cosmopolitanism proposes appreciating the common humanity in diverse peoples and recognizing an individual's part of a larger, connected world (Todd, 2009). Robustly theorized, the findings of cosmopolitanism offer insights into the dynamics of and potential strategies for reading cross-culturally. While much cosmopolitan theory notes the tension between the local and the global—the same tensions at play in reading international literature, more recently, scholars have argued for the importance of the local in cosmopolitanism.

If cosmopolitanism means letting go of local understandings (Calhoun, 2002), many critics contend that cosmopolitanism "might result in the abstraction of pupils from their particularistic histories and emotional ties" (Peterson, 2012, p. 238). This conflict between regional loyalties and cosmopolitanism lies at the heart of cosmopolitan education. In attempting to reconcile local loyalties with cosmopolitanism, many cosmopolitan theorists propose understanding cosmopolitanism through local and personal experiences (Wahlström, 2014). With this recognition of the importance of unique experiences, theorists contend with an understanding of cosmopolitanism that is not just theoretical but makes sense in the real world.

Noel Gough (2000) argues that the homogenizing effects of globalization can be resisted by emphasizing the performative, rather than the representational, aspects of curriculum work. That is, a better understanding of the high-minded ideals of cosmopolitanism can be achieved by focusing on the concrete rather than abstract. She points out that Gothic cathedral making, Polynesian navigation, modern cartography, and Indonesian rice farming, for example, can each be understood better performatively than conceptually. That is, cultures and concepts can be understood best through their particular examples; cosmopolitanism can similarly occur only through one's contact with a specific culture. "People can't love humanity in general, but only particular people," one observer noted. "Global relations are always encountered locally" (Donald, 2007, p. 291). In other words, there can be no cosmopolitan without the local. "There are only local universalisms and, for that matter, only 'local cosmopolitanisms,'" Lazarus maintains (2011, p. 134).

These debates point out a central aporia, or inherent contradiction, in cosmopolitanism, as pointed out by Derrida (Todd, 2009) and others: conditional hospitality requires a certain degree of hostility to the other (Koczanovicz, 2010). Negotiating cultural difference always risks the possibility of rejection. There can be no hospitality without hostility, no welcome without the limit to that welcome (Langmann, 2011). Teaching global citizenship with the assumption that the other is known "forecloses the possibility of welcoming" (Langmann, 2011, p. 399). If cosmopolitanism requires openness to another culture, then cosmopolitanism also requires a certain degree of uncertainty with regard to the alien culture, because unconditional hospitality does not exist.

Because of the potential for inherent antagonism between universal values and an individual's local culture, cosmopolitanism has sometimes been perceived as a threat to democracy (Koczanowicz, 2010) and patriotism (Nussbaum, 1994). If a cosmopolitan's allegiance is to universal values, how can he or she maintain allegiances to his or her country or locality? Even Nussbaum agrees: there is no "single moral world" (as cited in Hansen, 2010a, p. 154). Such threats to a reader's culture emerges, for example, when texts raise questions of cultural relativity. In Gaudelli's study of approaches to global studies, he described teachers' struggles with teaching lessons on genital mutilation, foot binding, polygamy, infanticide, and wife beating. A cosmopolitan perspective requires students to be open to the practices of an alien culture; however, certain practices compelled students to remain true to their culture's norms (Gaudelli, 2003). This tension between local loyalties and cosmopolitanism, an ideal of open-minded liberals, lies at the center of much debate on cosmopolitanism and should be of interest to anyone trying to get students to read cross culturally. While I am interested in a rooted cosmopolitanism (Appiah, 2005, 2006), scholars also assert there is no "single moral world" (Nussbaum as cited in Hansen, 2009, p. 154). With this, how can cultures remain faithful to themselves while rethinking of themselves in relation to others?

Several scholars have proposed an understanding of cosmopolitanism that brings together both the local and the global. Koczanowicz (2010) proposes a "dialogic cosmopolitanism," in which the main principle is to find out more about the complicated relationship between divergent points of views. Karim (2012) similarly argues that both globalism and tribalism are essential to maintain identity, and suggests several strategies to encourage the balance of globalism and tribalism in the classroom. This view of cosmopolitanism can be seen in a study done shortly after 9/11, in which the young people involved "demonstrated multiple and dynamic identities embracing local, national, and international perspectives." The study found that young people had multiple, flexible points of view toward the local and the global, and did not choose between a national or cosmopolitan outlook (Osler & Starkey, 2003).

Complicating the tension between the local and global are complications within an individual's identity. Beginning with the 1990s, a new cosmopolitanism emerged that emphasized the importance of cultural pluralism. It formed in reaction to classic cosmopolitanism, which seems to be premised in the idea cultural purity (Hansen, 2009), and to theorists who maintain that people inhabit "one and only one community." This new view of cosmopolitanism acknowledges "the unfathomable variability in human beings and their communities" and the need to attend to "new hybrid social configurations" that result from the intermingling of people, ideas, and activities in many parts of the world (Calhoun, 2002, p. 879).

In contrast to those who viewed patriotism as being in opposition to cosmopolitanism, many have pointed out the complexity of identity.

"We all belong to several communities simultaneously," Narayan pointed out (1993, p. 676). In Narayan's self-study, she found that, as a researcher, she was both an insider and outsider to the culture, which she studied, sometimes called upon to represent the West and sometimes identified as a "native." Indeed, identities are complicated; they are much more complicated than the patriotism vs. cosmopolitanism binary, much more complicated than even the nesting circles of self, family, neighborhood, city, and country, which Nussbaum imagines as illustrating cosmopolitanism. Nussbaum notes that scholars can "easily add to this list groupings based on ethnic, linguistic, historical, professional, gender, and sexual identities," (1994, para. 13), but Nussbaum does not acknowledge that these allegiances sometimes overlap and come into conflict with one another. Contrary to Nussbaum's assertion that the different parts of an individual's identity can be "easily add[ed]," negotiating these allegiances, Narayan points out, can be difficult.

Complexity of identity aside, it is nevertheless true that students can gain a richer understanding of themselves by interacting with other cultures (Hansen, 2010a; Nussbaum, 1994). In one study, Peruvian writers who immersed themselves in a European artistic tradition found this encounter with the "other" helpful in articulating their own vision and "com[ing] to a richer awareness of … [their own] traditions" (as cited in Hansen, 2010b, p. 12). Although cosmopolitanism may risk the possibility of hostility, a cosmopolitan outlook can promote a richer understanding of the self.

Many agree that cultivating a cosmopolitan outlook means rooting students in their lived experience (Hansen, 2009; Hansen, 2010a; Hansen, 2010b; Koh, 2008; Lingard, Nixon, & Ranson, 2008; Nussbaum, 1994). Deparochializing education is about "opening up boundaries and 'looking' outwards rather than inwards … but also demands deep connectedness with the local," Koh maintains (as cited in Lingard et al., 2008, p. 41). Articulating one of the main conflicts in cosmopolitanism, Koh argues that students must remain rooted in their local allegiances in order to be cosmopolitan. Schools can promote cosmopolitanism by cultivating a "community of enquirers … in which meanings would be continuously related to students' life worlds," write Lingard, Nixon, and Ranson (2008, p. 24). Educators can only promote a cosmopolitan perspective by connecting content to students' real life experiences. The conflict between students' local allegiances and deparochializing education constitutes one of the major themes in cosmopolitan education, and theorists agree that cosmopolitanism does not mean giving up an individual's local allegiances (Nussbaum, 1994). In fact, it can enhance them. But how can educators promote cosmopolitanism while supporting students' local allegiances? And how can they attend to students' multiple and conflicting identities?

David Hansen's cosmopolitanism "on the ground" offers a useful framework for balancing the cosmopolitan goals of education with the practical needs of the teachers and students in our class (Hansen, 2010b). Cosmopolitanism on the ground also known as cosmopolitanism from the ground up or "actually existing cosmopolitanism" (Hansen, 2010b, para. 11) recognizes the importance of local socialization but also acknowledges that cosmopolitan outlooks trigger a critical attitude toward tradition and customs. Cosmopolitanism on the ground recognizes that it is impossible to be cosmopolitan without a sense of the local. This philosophy aspires to be universal without being universalistic, local without being parochial (Hansen, 2010b). It is characterized by a receptivity to the new coinciding with a maintenance of loyalty to the known.

Cosmopolitanism on the ground differs from previous understandings of cosmopolitanism in that it recognizes:

1. the importance of local socialization as making education itself possible,
2. that cosmopolitan outlooks trigger a critical attitude toward tradition and customs, and
3. that curricula across all subjects can be cosmopolitan.

While the first tenet of cosmopolitanism on the ground finds socialization synonymous with education itself, and is thereby inextricable from discussions on cosmopolitan pedagogy, Hansen's second point makes clear that cosmopolitanism on the ground can engender a critical attitude toward traditions and customs, not just of an individual's own culture but of other cultures or representations of those cultures as well. Just as others have identified the importance of a critical, philosophical approach when broaching issues related to cultures (Choo, 2013; Gaudelli, 2003), a practical cosmopolitanism requires discussion and reflection.

Cosmopolitanism on the ground is part of a growing body of scholarship, which maintains that the local and the global are not in contention with but contingent upon one another (Appiah, 1998; Forte, Roberts, Murray, & Gray, 2002; Rizvi, 2014; Rizvi & Beech, 2017; Sobe, 2008; Sobe & Kowalczyk, 2012; Werbner, 2008). For Kwame Appiah, cosmopolitanism can only emerge in an individual with "membership in morally and emotionally significant communities" (Appiah as cited in Werbner, 2008, p. 15). It is through specific experiences that cosmopolitanism can be contextualized and "made meaningful to the lives of students" (Rizvi & Beech, 2017, p. 129). Cosmopolitanism, in other words, cannot exist as an abstraction; it must emerge in a specific locality and experience. For Forte, "locality/community/ethnicity" is "forged *in and through* [Forte's emphasis] rather than against these global processes" (Forte et al., 2002, p. 477). The local and global do not oppose one another or occupy distinct levels of a hierarchy. Rather, emblems of regional identity can become cosmopolitan when taken up by another group (Forte et al., 2002). In Forte's example, it is the simultaneous recognition of sameness *and* differences that enables cosmopolitanism. This recognition of both sameness and difference is also inherent in Hansen's cosmopolitanism on the ground, which insists one can be cosmopolitan while maintaining a critical attitude toward another culture.

This book illustrates ways in which teachers can *leverage* students' local and regional understandings and engender cosmopolitanism in educational contexts by making connections to students' lived experiences. The teachers here did this by leveraging students' religious, ethnic, and personal experiences.

Simply reading international literature does not itself necessarily engender cosmopolitanism. *Engaging* with international literature, however, promotes many attributes of cosmopolitanism including reflexivity, hospitality, intercultural dialogue, and cultural exchange (Wahlström, 2014).

References

Allan, M. (2007). Reading with one eye, speaking with one tongue: On the problem of address in world literature. *Comparative Literature Studies*, *44*(1–2), 1–19.

Appiah, K. A. (2005). *The ethics of identity*. Princeton, NJ: Princeton University Press.

Appiah, K. A. (2006). *Cosmopolitanism: Ethics in a world of strangers*. New York, NY: W. W. Norton.

Appiah, K. W. (1998). Cosmopolitan patriots. In P. Cheah & B. Robbins (Eds.), *Cosmopolitics: Thinking and feeling beyond the nation* (pp. 91–116). Minneapolis, MN: University of Minnesota Press.

Applebee, A., & Littell, M. (2006). *The Language of Literature: World Literature*. Evanston, IL: McDougall Littell.

Banks, J. (1993). Multicultural education: Historical development, dimensions, and practice. *Review of Research in Education*, *19*(3), 3–49.

Banks, J. (1994). *An introduction to multicultural education*. Boston, MA: Allyn and Bacon.

Beers, K. (2006). *Elements of literature: World literature*. Austin, TX: Holt, Rinehart and Winston.

Bingen, M. (2002). From archetypes to xenophobia: World literature is the "rite" stuff. *English Journal*, *91*(5), 40–45.

Bloom, A. (1987). *The closing of the American mind: How higher education has failed democracy and impoverished the souls of today's students*. New York, NY: Simon & Schuster.

Boglatz, J. (2005). *Talking race in the classroom*. New York, NY: Teachers College Press.

Bowler, E., Coe, B., McCollum, D., Fried, P., Ackley, K., Hausmann, E., & Mahoney, M. (1996). *Prentice Hall Literature: World masterpieces*, 4th Edition. Upper Saddle River, NJ: Prentice Hall.

Bryan, A. (2009). The intersectionality of nationalism and multiculturalism in the Irish curriculum: Teaching against racism? *Race Ethnicity and Education*, *12*(3), 297–317.

Cai, M. (2003a). Multiple definitions of multicultural literature: Is the debate really just "ivory tower" bickering? In D. Fox & K. Short (Eds.), *Stories matter: The complexity of cultural authenticity in children's literature* (pp. 269–283). Urbana, IL: National Council of Teachers of English.

Cai, M. (2003b). Can we fly across cultural gaps on the wings of imagination?: Ethnicity, experience, and cultural authenticity. In D. Fox & K. Short. (Eds.), *Stories matter: The complexity of cultural authenticity in children's literature* (pp. 167–181). Urbana, IL: National Council of Teachers of English.

Calhoun, C. (2002). The class consciousness of frequent travelers: Toward a critique of actually existing cosmopolitanism. *South Atlantic Quarterly*, *101*(4), 869–897.

Chappel, J. (2017). The trouble with reader response theory when reading multicultural literature: A critique of Dana Fox's and Kathy Short's *Stories Matter*. *Journal of Curriculum Theorizing*, *31*(3), 1–6.

Cheah, P. (2014). World against globe: Toward a normative conception of world literature. *New Literary History*, *45*(3), 303–329.

Choo, S. (2013). *Reading the world, the globe, and the cosmos: Approaches to teaching literature for the twenty-first century.* New York, NY: Peter Lang.

Choo, S. (2014). Cultivating a hospitable imagination: Re-envisioning the world literature curriculum through a cosmopolitan lens. *Curriculum Inquiry, 44*(1), 68–89.

Cooppan, V. (2009). The ethics of world literature: Reading others, reading otherwise. In D. Damrosch (Ed.), *Teaching world literature* (pp. 34–43). New York, NY: The Modern Language Association of America.

Crocco, M. (2005). Teaching *Shabanu*: The challenges of using world literature in the US social studies classroom. *Journal of Curriculum Studies, 37*(5), 561–582.

Damrosch, D. (2003). *What is world literature?* Princeton and Oxford: Princeton University Press.

Damrosch, D. (Ed.). (2009). *Teaching world literature.* New York, NY: The Modern Language Association of America.

Damrosch, D., & Spivak, G. C. (2011). Comparative literature/world literature: A discussion with Gayatri Chakravorty Spivak and David Damrosch. *Comparative Literature Studies, 48*(4), 455–485.

Donald, J. (2007). Internationalization, diversity and the humanities curriculum: Cosmopolitanism and multiculturalism revisited. *Journal of Philosophy of Education, 41*(3), 289–308.

Downing, K. (2002). Travelers, not tourists: A world literature curriculum. *English Journal, 91*(5), 46–51.

Dudley-Marling, C. (2003). "I'm not from Pakistan": Multicultural literature and the problem of representation. In D. Fox & K. Short (Eds.), *Stories matter: The complexity of cultural authenticity in children's literature* (pp. 3–24). Urbana, IL: National Council of Teachers of English.

Dunn, S. (2001). On the convergence of myth and reality: Examples from the Pacific Islands. *The Geographical Journal, 167*(2), 125–138.

Dressel, J. H. (2005). Personal response and social responsibility: Responses of middle school students to multicultural literature. *Journal of Adolescent and Adult Literacy, 58*(8), 750–764.

Fang, Z., Fu, D., & Lamme, L. L. (2003). The trivialization and misuse of multicultural literature: Issues of representation and communication. In D. Fox & K. Short (Eds.), *Stories matter: The complexity of cultural authenticity in children's literature* (pp. 284–303). Urbana, IL: National Council of Teachers of English.

Forte, M., Roberts, M., Murray, D., Gray, J., & Dept. of Anthropology. (2002). *Re-engineering indigeneity: Cultural brokerage, the political economy of tradition, and the Santa Rosa Carib community of Arima, Trinidad & Tobago* (Doctoral Dissertation). National Library of Australia.

Foster, J. (2009). Cultural encounters in global contexts: World literature as a one-semester general education course. In D. Damrosch (Ed.), *Teaching world literature* (pp. 155–164). New York, NY: The Modern Language Association of America.

Foucault, M. (1969). What is an author? Retrieved from http://www.movementresearch.org/classesworkshops/melt/Foucault_WhatIsAnAuthor.pdf

Fox, D., & Short, K. G. (2003). The complexity of cultural authenticity in children's literature: Why the debates really matter. In D. Fox & K. Short (Eds.), *Stories matter: The complexity of cultural authenticity in children's literature* (pp. 3–24). Urbana, IL: National Council for Teachers of English.

Friedman, T. (2005). *The world is flat: A brief history of the twenty-first century*. New York, NY: Picador/Farrar, Straus and Giroux.

Gaudelli, W. (2003). *World class: Teaching and learning in global times*. Mahwah, NJ: Lawrence Erlbaum Associates.

Gough, N. (2000). Locating curriculum studies in the global village. *Journal of Curriculum Studies, 32*(2), 329–42.

Hansen, D. T. (2009). Dewey and cosmopolitanism. *Education and Culture, 25*(2), 126–140.

Hansen, D. T. (2010a). Chasing butterflies without a net: Interpreting cosmopolitanism. *Studies in Philosophy and Education, 29*(2), 151–166.

Hansen, D. T. (2010b). Cosmopolitanism and education: A view from the ground. *Teachers College Record, 112*(1), 1–30.

Hirsch, E. D. (1988). *Cultural literacy: What every American needs to know*. New York, NY: Vintage Books.

Jordan, S., & Purves, A. C. (1993). *Issues in the responses of students to culturally diverse texts: A preliminary study*. New York, NY: National Research Center on Literature Teaching & Learning.

Kaomea, J. (2006). Nā wāhine mana: A postcolonial reading of classroom discourse on the imperial rescue of oppressed Hawaiian women. *Pedagogy, Culture and Society, 14*(3), 329–348.

Karim, S. (2012). The co-existence of globalism and tribalism: A review of the literature. *Journal of Research in International Education, 11*(2), 137–151.

Kerschner, L. (2002). Teaching world literature: Preparing global citizens. *English Journal, 91*(5), 76–81.

Kim, E. (1976). *A survey of Asian American literature: Social perspectives* (Doctoral dissertation). University of California, Berkeley, American Literature.

Kim, E. (1982). *Asian American literature: An introduction to writings and their social contexts*. Philadelphia, PA: Temple University Press.

Koczanowicz, L. (2010). Cosmopolitanism and its predicaments. *Studies in Philosophy and Education, 29*(2), 141–149.

Koh, A. (2008). Deparochializing education: Re-envisioning education in ASEAN. In B. Lingard, J. Nixon, & S. Ranson (Eds.), *Transforming learning in schools and communities: The remaking of education for a cosmopolitan society* (pp. 37–49). New York, NY: Continuum Books.

Langmann, E. (2011). Representational and territorial economies in global citizenship education: Welcoming the other at the limit of cosmopolitan hospitality. *Globalisation, Societies and Education, 9*(3–4), 399–409.

Lawall, S. (1994). *Reading world literature: Theory, history, and practice*. Austin, TX: University of Texas Press.

Lawall, S. (2009). The west and the rest: Frames for reading world literature. In D. Damrosch (Ed.), *Teaching World Literature* (pp. 17–33). New York, NY: The Modern Language Association.

Lazarus, N. (2011). Cosmopolitanism and the specificity of the local in world literature. *The Journal of Commonwealth Literature*, *46*(1), 119–137.

Lehman, B. A., Freeman, E. B., & Scharer, P. L. (2010). *Reading globally, K-8: Connecting students to the world through literature.* Thousand Oaks, CA: Corwin.

Lingard, B., Nixon, J., & Ranson, S. (2008). Remaking education for a globalized world: Policy and pedagogic possibilities. In B. Lingard, J. Nixon, & S. Ranson (Eds.), *Transforming learning in schools and communities: The remaking of education for a cosmopolitan society* (pp. 3–36). New York, NY: Continuum Books.

Loh, C. E. (2009). Reading the world: Reconceptualizing reading multicultural literature in the English language arts classroom in a global world. *Changing English: Studies in culture & education*, *16*(3), 287–299.

Loutzenheiser, L. W. (1996). How schools play "smear the queer." *Feminist Teacher*, *10*(2), 59–64.

Loutzenheiser, L. W., & MacIntosh, L. B. (2004). Citizenships, sexualities, and education. *Theory Into Practice*, *43*(2), 151–158.

Malik, K. (2013). *Multiculturalism and its discontents: Re-thinking diversity after 9/11.* London: Seagull Books.

Moll, L. C. (1994). Mediating knowledge between homes and classrooms. In D. Keller-Cohen (Ed.), *Literacy: Interdisciplinary conversations* (pp. 385–410). Cresskill, NJ: Hampton Press.

Monseau, V. (2002). From the editor. *English Journal*, *91*(5), 1.

Moulton, R. G. (1911). *World literature and its place in general culture.* New York, NY: Palgrave Macmillan.

Nandi, S. (2013). Reading the "other" in world literature: Toward a discourse of unfamiliarity. In M. A. Raja, H. Stringer, & Z. Vandezande (Eds.), *Critical pedagogy and global literature: Worldly teaching* (pp. 75–96). New York, NY: Palgrave Macmillan.

Narayan, K. (1993). How native is a "native" anthropologist? *American Anthropologist*, *95*(3), 671–686.

Needham, A. D. (2009). The place of difference in cross-cultural literacy. In D. Damrosch (Ed.), *Teaching World Literature* (pp. 73–85). New York, NY: The Modern Language Association of America.

Nikola-Lisa, W. (2003). "Around my table" is not always enough. In D. Fox & K. Short (Eds.), *Stories matter: The complexity of cultural authenticity in children's literature* (pp. 46–49). Urbana, IL: National Council of Teachers of English.

Nussbaum, M. (1994). Patriotism and cosmopolitanism. *Boston Review*. Retrieved from http://bostonreview.net/martha-nussbaum-patriotism-and-cosmopolitanism

Osler, A., & Starkey, H. (2003). Learning for cosmopolitan citizenship: Theoretical debates and young people's experiences. *Educational Review*, *55*(3), 243–254.

Pang, V. (2001). *Multicultural education: A caring-centered, reflective approach* (1st ed.). Boston, MA: McGraw-Hill.

Peterson, A. (2012). The educational limits of ethical cosmopolitanism: Towards the importance of virtue in cosmopolitan education and communities. *British Journal of Educational Studies, 60*(3), 227–242.

Pizer, J. (2006). *The idea of world literature: History and pedagogical practice.* Baton Rouge, LA: Louisiana State University.

Puchner, M. et al. (2012). *The Norton anthology of world literature: Volumes A–F.* New York, NY: W. W. Norton & Company.

Qualifications and Curriculum Authority. (2006). Teaching world literature in the primary school: A discussion paper. *QCA Reading differences project.* Retrieved from http://217.35.77.12/archive/england/papers/education/pdfs/QCA-06-2444_Discussion_paper.pdf

Reese, J. (2002). Learning for understanding: The role of world literature. *English Journal, 91*(5), 63–69.

Richardson, T. (2011). At the garden gate: Community building through food: Revisiting the critique of "food, folk, and fun" in multicultural education. *Urban Review, 43,* 107–123.

Rizvi, F. (2014). *Encountering education in the global.* London & New York: Routledge.

Rizvi, F., & Beech, J. (2017). Global mobilities and the possibilities of a cosmopolitan curriculum. *Curriculum Inquiry, 47*(1), 125–134.

Robertson, R. T. (1974). A work of global status: A new reading curriculum in English.

Rose, M. G. (1996). The translator and the voice of the other: A case in point. In T. Carroll (Ed.), *No small world: Visions and revisions of world literature* (pp. 20–33). Urbana, IL: National Council of Teachers of English.

Sartre, J. P. (1965). *What is literature*? (B. Frenchtman, Trans.). New York, NY: Harper & Row.

Shankar, S. (2012). *Flesh and fish blood: Postcolonialism, translation, and vernacular.* Berkeley, CA: University of California Press.

Shankar, S. (2013). Introduction to the symposium. Proceedings from *Words in the World Symposium.* Honolulu, HI: University of Hawai'i. Retrieved from http://hdl.handle.net/10125/29716

Shankar, S. (2014). Professor, University of Hawai'i English Department. Personal Interview.

Shin, K. S. (2011). *Please look after mom.* New York, NY: Alfred A. Knopf.

Short, K. G. (2012). Story as world making. *Language Arts, 90*(1), 9–17.

Short, K. G., Day, D., & Schroeder, J. (2016). *Teaching globally: Reading the world through literature.* Portland, ME: Stenhouse.

Short, K. G., Evans, A., & Hildebrand, K. (2011, August/September). Celebrating international books in today's classrooms: The notable books for a global society award. *Reading Today,* 34–36.

Sleeter, C., & Grant, C. A. (1999). *Making choices for multicultural education : Five approaches to race, class, and gender* (3rd ed.). Upper Saddle River, NJ: Merrill.

Smith, A. (2006). *The color of violence: The INCITE! anthology.* Cambridge, MA: South End Press.

Smith, K. (2011). What good is world literature: Pedagogy and the rhetoric of moral crisis. *College English, 73*(6), 585–603.

Spencer, M. (1994). In the canon's mouth: Being lucid about the local. In S. Lawall (Ed.), *Reading world literature: Theory, history, and literature* (pp. 328–350). Austin, TX: University of Texas Press.

Spivak, G. (2003). *Death of a discipline*. New York, NY: Columbia University Press.

Spivak, G. (2009). Rethinking comparativism. *New Literary History, 40*(3), 609–626.

Sobe, W. N. (2008). *Provincializing the worldly citizen: Yugoslav student and teacher travel and Slavic cosmopolitanism in the internet era*. New York, NY: Peter Lang.

Sobe, W. N., & Kowalczyk, J. (2012). The problem of context in comparative education research. *ECPS – Educational, Cultural and Psychological Studies, 3*(6), 55–74.

Sung, Y. K., & Meyer, R. J. (2011). Rethinking cultural authenticity in global literature: A Korean example. In R. J. Meyer & K. F. Whitmore (Eds.), *Reclaiming reading: Teachers, students, and researchers regaining spaces for thinking and action* (pp. 163–166). London: Routledge, Taylor, & Francis Group.

Tan, A. (2003). *The opposite of fate*. New York, NY: G. P. Putnam's Son.

Thomas, L. (2007). When literature discussion seems to go nowhere: Reevaluating teaching and learning. *WOW Stories: Connections from the Classrooms, 1*(1). Retrieved from http://wowlit.org/on-line-publications/

Todd, S. (2009). *Toward an imperfect education: Facing humanity, rethinking cosmopolitanism*. Boulder, CO: Paradigm.

Top 100 world literature titles. Perfection Learning. https://www.perfectionlearning.com/catalog/category/view/s/top-100-world-literature-titles/id/1663/

Venuti, L. (2009). Teaching in translation. In D. Damrosch (Ed.), *Teaching World Literature*. New York, NY: The Modern Language Association of America.

wa Thiong'o, N. (1981). *Decolonising the mind: The politics of language in African literature*. Portsmouth, NH: Heinemann Educational Books.

wa Thiong'o, N. (2012). *Globalectics: Theory and the politics of knowing*. New York, NY: Columbia University Press.

Wagner, T. (2008). *The global achievement gap: Why even our best schools don't teach the new survival skills our children need—and what we can do about it*. New York, NY: Basic Books.

Wahlström, N. (2014). Toward a conceptual framework for understanding cosmopolitanism on the ground. *Curriculum Inquiry, 44*(1), 113–132.

Werbner, P. (Ed.). (2008). *Anthropolgy and the new cosmopolitanism: Rooted, feminist, and vernacular perspectives*. Oxford, UK: Berg.

Chapter Two

My Own Experience Teaching World Literature

Given the numerous definitions of World Literature in circulation, it should not be surprising that my own World Literature curriculum experienced several permutations. First following a mandated curriculum, I taught curricula I did not recognize as World Literature. Eventually, when I became lead teacher, I taught the "Great Works" version of World Literature dominated by the Western canon. Finally, I revamped my curriculum to reflect literature from a diversity of countries. Each iteration proved unsatisfactory in different ways. Balancing an interest in global coverage with the need for student engagement forced me to reflect on my implicit and explicit learning objectives and to find the sweet spot where international coverage and student engagement converged.

American Literature as World Literature

For several years, I taught a World Literature class that was not particularly worldly. The reading list included *Night* by Elie Wiesel, *The*

House on Mango Street by Sandra Cisneros, *Twelfth Night* by William Shakespeare, and *The Catcher in the Rye* by J. D. Salinger.

The list embraced a dizzying mix of traditionally American literature (Salinger), literature by ethnic Americans (Cisneros), British Literature (Shakespeare), and only one title that might be considered non-British or non-American (Wiesel). The class wasn't so much a survey of World Literature as it was a survey of American literature with a couple non-American texts included in the mix. It wasn't until the spring that I even realized the course was a course in World Literature.

Frankly, I didn't care what part of the world the texts came from. I cared only that the kids were engaged and challenged. That was a hard enough task without worrying about whether or not I was covering "the world." So *Twelfth Night,* which properly belonged in a course on British Literature, had them laughing at five hundred year old puns through the arduous month of May. Halleluah!

However unsatisfying the World Literature list may have been to me personally, it proved engaging for many of the students in my class. Told through rich, mysterious and evocative language, *A House on Mango Street* opened itself up to lessons on close readings and high-level discussions on the use of language. The vignettes about protective fathers and abusive relationships were relevant and interesting to young girls in the midst of adolescence. And because the vignettes were short, the students were able to make their way through the cloaked language.

Night, a compelling memoir told of dramatic events and introduced the internal conflict of an author questioning his faith. Not a difficult read, the text proved accessible to students of varying reading abilities. Supplementary lessons on the Holocaust, which drew from the wealth of high-quality Holocaust curriculum on the market, provided more dramatic stories and lessons even though few to no students were Jewish.

Students had a hard time with *Catcher in the Rye,* not because it was set in New York, a place that was arguably foreign to my students. Rather, the students had difficulty making sense of the stream of consciousness style and non-chronological narrative.

This is not to say my students hated all difficult texts. Students loved *Twelfth Night* for its gender-bending humor. Based on their strong response, students were able to follow Shakespeare's play on words just fine. So successful was *Twelfth Night*, we saved it until the end of the year when we knew everyone was exhausted from the school year.

However successful some of the curriculum had been, when I was handed the course to develop as the lead teacher, I revamped the curriculum to include works I thought were more reflective of what I perceived as World Literature. I spent summers scouring bloated anthologies of World Literature, which included everything from the works of medieval Japan, to the Tao Te Ching, Zen parables, *Don Quixote, The Odyssey, Beowulf,* the Enuma Elish creation myth, the *Book of Job*, and excerpts from the *Bhagavad Gita.* As an Asian American, I had traveled abroad and had minored in Asian Studies. Nevertheless, having attended schools in America, I had been primarily schooled in literature written in English. As a result, many of the works outside of the British and American traditions were foreign to me; in many cases, they seemed impenetrable.

World Literature as Western Civilization

Another iteration of my World Literature course followed a "Great Works" paradigm dominated by great works of Western civilization. My sophomores read Edith Hamilton's abridged version of Homer's *The Odyssey*, Franz Kafka's *The Metamorphosis*, Sophocles' *Antigone*, Voltaire's *Candide*, and excerpts from Seamus Heaney's beautiful translation of *Beowulf*. *Antigone*, though short, presents the age-old debate between the rule of law and the rule of conscience. The text, an easy, straightforward read, opened itself up to questions my students were ready to ask. *Candide*, on the other hand, proved inaccessible even for my brightest sophomores. Even after showing them excerpts from Leonard Bernstein's operatic adaptation of the novella, my students did not relate to the dark humor of our hero from Westphalia. Edith Hamilton's abridged translation of *The Odyssey*, passed down to me by my department head, nevertheless managed to engage my students with stories of gods and goddesses, which many were familiar with from their middle school curriculum. *The Metamorphosis* they enjoyed for its absurdity and compelling, neurotic main character. But after a year of this curriculum, I asked myself: Why was I feeding my students a diet of dead white men? *In Hawai'i*?

World Literature as International Literature

In other iterations of the course, I made a concerted effort to incorporate more non-Western texts from outside the United States. My class read Ryunosuke Akutagawa's Japanese short story "In a Grove" (which inspired the Akiro Kurosawa film *Rashomon*). Written like a detective story, "In a Grove" spurred students to question character motivation and to guess the true story of what had happened in a rape and murder. Understanding the different points of views, however, required understanding Japanese idea of shame, among other cultural (and historical) factors. And although many of the students in my class were ethnically Japanese, far removed from mores of medieval Japan, the class and I had difficulty relating to the characters' reactions.

We read a dramatic chapter from the sprawling Indian epic the *Bhagavad Gita*. In the chapters, the god Krishna directs the protagonist Arjuna to kill his family members in battle. I had hoped the story would inspire discussions on the conflict between duty and morality and between cultural differences, but the actions of the characters didn't make sense to my students. Frankly, they didn't make sense to me, so our discussions fell short.

Our unit on Chinua Achebe's *Things Fall Apart*, an easy read that provided the necessary context to understand the story, proved successful as it has in so many classrooms. Students were able to engage with the father and son dynamics even though the story was set in a place where people drank wine from human skulls. Written in response to texts like *Heart of Darkness* and *Mister Johnson*, which portrayed Nigeria inaccurately from an outsiders' point of view, Achebe wrote *Things Fall Apart* in response to what he saw as racist portrayals of his countrymen. He had an interest in sharing the stories of Nigeria with fidelity to a western audience. *Things Fall Apart* represented the kind of text I wanted to include more of in my international literature curriculum, but Achebe happened to know English from having grown up in a mission where English language was taught and spoken (Achebe & Brooks, 1994). Not all international literature would be written in English expressly for a Western audience.

Despite a few successes, I found I was unprepared to teach many of these international works. While I was happy with the selections and lessons in the other classes I taught, for my World Literature class I felt I had only scratched the surface of these texts and the cultures and authors they represented.

Conclusion

My experience illustrates many of the challenges of teaching cross culturally, itemized in Chapter 1. A lack of teacher training as well as the enormous scope of World Literature contributed to a lack of confidence that, in turn, contributed to poor World Literature instruction. While a lack of good translations from non-English-language literature is widely cited as one of the major impediments to teaching World Literature, the lack of teacher resources created another obstacle to teaching World Literature. While a glut of resources existed, for example, on *The Tempest* and the Holocaust, I discovered a lack of educational resources, including high-quality multimodal resources, such as posters, videos, and digital resources or activities on the *Bhagavad Gita* and the Hawaiian creation story the *Kumulipo.* This lack of resources also contributed to an inability to teach these texts well.

Bright Spot

One of the most successful lessons in my final iteration of the course was a lesson on Gabriel Garcia Marquez's "A Very Old Man with Enormous Wings." In this popular, translated short story, a strange old man bearing giant wings appears in a small town. Although the townspeople immediately believe he is an angel, they nevertheless treat him poorly, pelting him with stones, and even consider killing him.

A simple story that offers students an example of magical realism, the story ignited far more discussion than I had anticipated. When I raised the question, "What does the old man represent?" I inadvertently raised a number of issues and questions about angels, which the Catholic school students in the class were familiar with and interested in. Although only half of the students at the school were Catholic, by virtue of attending the school—which held monthly religious services, required four years of Religion coursework, and generally immersed their students in Catholic culture through prayer and observation of religious holidays, the students in my class had more than average knowledge of angels.

One student made the connection between the old man and the Angel Gabriel, who appears in both the Old and New Testaments and was known for being a messenger. With this comment, this student demonstrated knowledge of angels and insights into the text, far surpassing my own. Other students chimed in with their understanding of what angels were and how angels worked. Were they real? And did the presence of angels indicate the presence of God himself? The discussion, which I thought would last twenty minutes, ended up taking the whole hour, with students personally invested in whether the old man was an angel and, if so, what this meant.

Drawing upon students' funds of knowledge as students attending a Catholic school, the story made connections to ideas students cared about. I had presented the story before in another, secular school, also with positive results, but not to the extent I saw at this Catholic school. Engaging to students from a variety of backgrounds, the story piqued particular interest among the students at a Catholic school.

At the time I gave the lesson, I saw the connection between the content of the story and the latent background knowledge my students held. However, it had not occurred to me that this might be a strategy to engage students with international literature. It was only after speaking with a number of World Literature teachers and seeing again and again, the importance of the local in teaching the global, that I saw the importance of making connections to students' contexts even when teaching international literature.

What follows are three teacher stories of their experiences engaging students with international literature by making connections to students' identities and contexts. Together, they demonstrate ways teachers can leverage students' parochial experiences to access the sometimes foreign and disorienting stories in international literature.

Reference

Achebe, C., & Brooks, J. (1994). Chinua Achebe, the art of fiction no. 139. *The Paris Review*. https://www.theparisreview.org/interviews/1720/chinua-achebe-the-art-of-fiction-no-139-chinua-achebe

Literary Works Cited

Achebe, Chinua. (1958). *Things Fall Apart.*
Akutagawa, Ryunosuke. (1922). "In a Grove."
Cary, Joyce. (1939). *Mister Johnson.*
Cisneros, Sandra. (1984). *The House on Mango Street.*
Conrad, Joseph. (1899). *Heart of Darkness.*
de Cervantes, Miguel. (1605). *Don Quixote.*
Hamilton, Edith. (1942). *Mythology: Timeless Tales of Gods and Heroes.*
Heaney, Seamus. (2000). *Beowulf.*
Kafka, Franz. (1915). *The Metamorphosis.*
Marquez, Gabriel Garcia. (1968). "A Very Old Man with Enormous Wings."
Shakespeare, William. (1623). *Twelfth Night.*
Salinger, J. D. (1951). *The Catcher in the Rye.*
Shakespeare, William. (1623). *The Tempest.*
Sophocles. (1623). *Antigone.*
Voltaire. (1759). *Candide.*
Vyasa. *Bhagavad Gita.*
Wiesel, Elie. (1955). *Night.*

Chapter Three

Engendering Cosmopolitanism Through Shared Personal Experience

The Case of University Laboratory School

The case of University Laboratory School (Lab School) illustrates the enormous difficulties of internationalizing curricula. With a team of highly qualified teachers, dedicated to the goal of broadening the school's curriculum beyond British/US-centric texts, the school worked for over thirty years to introduce its students to literature from Asia and the Pacific including Australia and throughout Europe and the Americas. Despite the department's concerted efforts, its most successful and enduring curriculum has been its literature of and about Hawai'i. Indeed, the high school has been recognized for its role in promoting and popularizing "local literature" of Hawai'i (Morikawa, 1994). Rather than broaden its curriculum to the various corners of the globe as it hoped to do, the school's efforts at internationalizing its curricula have resulted in a focus on "neighborhood literature." Their story reminds us of the importance of students' unique place-based experiences in engaging students. The case of Lab School nevertheless offers glimmers of hope for the possibilities of internationalizing curriculum and insights into ways teachers can connect the local and the global.

University Laboratory School

Originally established as an arm of the University of Hawai'i, the University Lab School, a K–12 institution serving just 450 students, was designed as a "real world laboratory" responsible for providing its students quality instruction while creating and publishing innovative curricula for the state. As a charter school that develops and implements original curricula, the University Lab School is unique in several aspects. Not only are teachers given the freedom to craft their curriculum as they see fit, teachers in the English department during the 1980s to the early 2000s were given time off to conduct research and develop their curriculum. These endeavors resulted in the publication of five textbooks edited by the teachers at the school.

Charged with inventing and testing educational programs, the school recruits students from a variety of different backgrounds, geographic locations, and academic abilities. "One third of our kids by design are below average ability. *By design*," said Bill Teter, veteran teacher at the school for over 30 years. Despite the diversity of its student body, the students tend to outperform other public schools in the area, "earn consistently high scores on standardized and other tests. Almost all of the graduates go on to post-secondary education" (School Website).

Bill Teter

Of Irish and German descent, Bill Teter moved to Hawai'i from the U.S. mainland in 1978, and in 1988, joined the English department at University Lab. With a Master's degree in English, Bill shared the department's interest in international literature. During his studies, he even considered pursuing Irish and Japanese literature.

Although committed to the project of internationalizing English language curriculum, Bill said lack of knowledge and limited time kept him from expanding his curriculum. At the time of our interviews, he taught twelfth grade European literature, including not only British but also French, German, Greco-Roman, and ancient Sumerian texts, with the rationale that the school considers those "part[s] of the world to be foundational to the literature that develops in the west," Bill said.

During his time at the school, Bill spearheaded and edited two anthologies: *Growing Up Local* (1998), an anthology of local literature by writers of Hawai'i, and *Hapai na Leo* (2010), an anthology of native Hawaiian authors.

Efforts to Internationalize Curriculum

With a vision of a more international Language Arts curriculum, since the 1980s, University's Lab English department has been committed to broadening its curriculum to include texts from all corners of the world. Rather than attempt to teach World Literature in a semester or year course as many schools do, University Lab divided its entire English program by geography as follows.

10th: Asian/Pacific and Local Literature
11th: Literature of the Americas
12th: British and European Literature

The tenth grade literature includes literature from Asia and the Pacific including India, New Zealand, and Hawaii. Middle Eastern, Greco-Roman, and Old English works are included in European literature. The American literature course includes literature from North, South, and Central America, not just the US. Africa was notably absent from the school's curriculum.

The teachers charged with teaching and creating the curriculum were all highly qualified. Department members held Master's degree or PhDs in English in addition to numerous years of teaching experience. Three of the department members ultimately stayed at the school for over thirty-five years; only one of the five teachers stayed for only sixteen years.

To achieve its goal of broadening its curriculum, over the past forty years, the school has published five textbooks:

- *Asian-Pacific Literature* (Volumes I–III) edited by James and Cheryl Harstad (1981)
- *British and European Literatures* (Volumes I–III) published with James and Cheryl Harstad (1983)
- *Growing Up Local: An Anthology of Poetry and Prose from Hawai'i* (1998) edited by James Harstad, Bill Teter, Eric Chock, and Darrell Lum

- *Literature of the Americas* edited by Lanning Lee and George Drick (2001)
- *Hapai na Leo* edited by Bill Teter (2010)

In order to research and prepare the anthologies, teachers were given significant time to research and even travel to develop their curriculum. Lanning Lee, editor of the Americas textbook, for example, spent summers in Canada, studying Canadian literature and connecting with local authors for source material. Lee, like the other teachers in the department, was allotted approximately 15–20 hours/week for reading and researching for the book, a project that took seven years.

Nevertheless, despite the department's hard work over thirty years, the main texts for the literature of the Americas, continue to be tried and true texts of the American canon, not too different from many other schools. According to the 2016–2017 Literature of the Americas syllabus, the major texts included:

- *Their Eyes Were Watching God* by Zora Neale Hurston
- *The Great Gatsby* by F. Scott Fitzgerald
- *The Grapes of Wrath* by John Steinbeck
- *The Catcher in the Rye* by J. D. Salinger

Although the department still implemented selections from the American literature anthology, the longer works, which students have the opportunity to engage with for an extended period of time, were not from Central or South American or Canada. They were from the United States.

Bill acknowledged the curriculum's continued focus on the west. "There's still primarily a Western emphasis," he lamented. "It's still a work in progress for us." He reasoned that some of the selections in the school's anthologies had become dated. With references students no longer understood, some of the selections had not stood the test of time. "We don't really use [the Asian Pacific literature text] anymore," Bill said. "It's really outdated ... written in the 50s and 60s. That was a long time ago. ... Some of the cultural references—pop culture stars of the 60s—those are relatively trivial hang-ups that some kids [stumble on]."

The school's most popular anthologies meanwhile have been anthologies of Hawai'i. Of the school's three-part anthology on literature of Asia and the Pacific, its most popular was Volume 1, which includes the literature of Hawai'i. Volumes II and III with selections from New Zealand, Australia, and Vietnam in contrast "tend not to sell as well," Bill said. When asked why, Bill pointed to the text and said, "That [pointing to Hawai'i]." Student readers took greater interest in literature by local Hawai'i writers, the school found.

Bill witnessed the same dynamic with the publication of *Growing Up Local*, an anthology of local literature. The anthology featured the constellation of talented local writers including Darrell Lum and Eric Chock, credited with launching "local literature"[1]; Cathy Song, already anthologized by Norton; and Lois-Ann Yamanaka, who would go on to publish numerous novels and receive national attention. Even the publisher of the anthology Wing-tek Lum acknowledged it was one of the press's "more successful anthologies." With five editions over eighteen years, the press sold nearly 17,000 copies of the book, many to public and private schools in Hawai'i (Lum email correspondence, 2016).

Able to relate to the stories and places of the stories about Hawai'i, some told in pidgeon English—the Hawaiian creole English unique to Hawai'i, *Growing Up Local* engaged readers familiar with the place. Bill's experience with *Asian-Pacific Literature* and *Growing up Local*, both of which were taken up by public schools in Hawai'i, illustrate the power of place-based learning.

While some of the anthologies were sold in the U.S. mainland, not surprisingly, the anthologies about Hawai'i proved popular mainly in Hawai'i. "There's just not that many people interested in local literature on the mainland," Bill said. "That's been our experience." While this trend might be seen as navel-gazing on the part of readers and students in Hawai'i, the same argument could be made for American readers who tend to eschew foreign texts.

Rather than discount the importance of local literature, Bill has tried to use local literature as a springboard to engage with international literature. "We've tried to celebrate neighborhood literature. … and go outward from there. So our students understand that the texts that they read by someone in a voice that they sort of recognize as their uncle or their dad or even their own. It's related. It's the same kind of creativity you'd find from someone writing in Japan or India or Great Britain," he said. "We do move out from the local to the more global."

One of the school's more successful lessons pairs local literature with global literature. "I think we've been most successful in that regard in our 11th grade text where we've taken in North and South American writers and paired them in the text itself with student writers, our students." In this lesson, instructors compared and contrasted the writing of students in Hawai'i—which students immediately engaged with, with texts thematically related to texts from North or South America, texts students had greater difficulty relating to. The student text situated in Hawai'i provided a means to connect the stories of the international text.

Bill himself admitted he sometimes preferred texts for very specific, idiosyncratic connections. In one instance, he found himself attracted to a text because he knew the specific house mentioned in the text:

> What I like about *The Surfers*, I know the house that takes place. I've been to that house. [The story's about] a Vietnam veteran who's dying in the back of Palolo Valley. I was in that house. When I read that story, I said, "I've been there."

Able to relate to the specific locality of the story, Bill was drawn into the story. It presents an example of the deeply personal nature of engagement and the importance of connecting to readers' lived experiences.

Despite the school's challenges at broadening its curriculum, Bill did experience success with his unit on the *Epic of Gilgamesh*. This long-standing unit in his twelfth grade curriculum went especially well one year when the tragic death of a classmate made the ancient Sumerian text particularly relevant for students.

Epic of Gilgamesh

Originally written in the Akkaddian language over 4,000 years ago, the twelve tablets of the *Epic of Gilgamesh* tell the story of Gilgamesh, the king of Mesopotamia. So hard a ruler is Gilgamesh, his people entreat the gods for help. Siding with the people, the gods send down Enkidu to curb Gilgamesh's harsh rule. Although Gilgamesh prevails in the battle, the two become close friends. The gods' lack of mercy for Gilgamesh does not end, however, and in Tablet Seven, Enkidu, now Gilgamesh friend and companion, dies. The tragic event spurs Gilgamesh to seek immortality, a goal he does not achieve. Instead, the book ends with a report of the underworld from Enkidu.

The oldest text to have survived anywhere in the world (Damrosch, 2003), the *Epic of Gilgamesh* shares a story of Assyrian-Babylonian Mesopotamia, one of the greatest civilizations of the ancient world. Found and translated by British archaeologists in the early 19th-century, the *Epic of Gilgamesh* has been described as the first true work of World Literature (2003).

Although written as a national poem to the Babylonians, similar to the epics of Homer, generations of scholars have taken great interest in the text. However, their particular interests have been informed by their unique time and place. Originally titled the "Chaldean Account of Genesis," early European readers were most interested in the Great Flood depicted in the text. Triangulated against the Biblical account of the flood and the Greek epic, it confirmed the historical veracity of these events that would be of interest to readers of the day.

Other translators of the time meanwhile read it in terms of "19th-century European ideals of national autonomy and nationality identity" (Damrosch, 2003, p. 64). Gilgamesh's theme of political despotism and the autonomy of its citizens spoke to British explorers whose country had just recently been established. While early British explorers and translators highlighted the aspects that would be most interesting to its English language readers, connecting the text to the lives of high school students is another story.

Bill engages students with the text by emphasizing its simple narrative strength and the experience of the loss of a loved one, which many student have experienced by the time they reach their senior year. Bill strives to have students appreciate reading as a pleasure in itself. He does this by making connections to students' lives. Essential questions include: How do you deal with death? How do you make sure you stick around after you die? "We think these are issues that different cultures explore in different ways," he said. "Millennia later, we read that and we are moved. We feel it."

While grief is certainly a universal theme, the unit on the *Epic of Gilgamesh* particularly resonated with his students one year when the tragic death of a classmate in a car accident made the text especially relevant. As a small school, everyone in the class knew the student who had died. Not a drunk driving accident and not caused by the student's own error, the student by all accounts had been a victim of someone else's careless mistake. The student's life had been abruptly cut short for no meaningful reason. Reading the *Epic of Gilgamesh* became a lesson in understanding death, reflecting on the nature of indifferent gods, and ultimately coming to terms and obtaining closure over their friend's death. "When we read of Enkidu's death," Bill explained, "when Gilgamesh explains his lament, when he tells the gods, 'I don't want to understand. I want my friend back,' that resonates with these kids in this very different time and world."

Despite the fact that the text predated students by four of five millennia—a culture far removed from the contexts of his students, Bill's students "were silenced." The text provided a powerful springboard for students to see their feelings enacted in literature, and through discussion students were able to express their own feelings.

Bill's lesson on the *Epic of Gilgamesh* was made possible in part by the fact that he had read the epic in high school himself. This positive encounter, which engendered a familiarity and comfort with the text, helped facilitate the successful implementation of the text. This example points out the cyclical nature of high school curriculum. Informed by their own high school experiences, even teachers looking to internationalize their curriculum teach what they know.

Conclusion

The case of University Lab School offers a startling example of the enormous difficulty of internationalizing curriculum. Given time to conduct research and create curriculum over a period of thirty years, the English teachers charged with expanding the school's curriculum found they best engaged their students through "neighborhood literature." The school's three-volume collections in European and Asia-Pacific literature have been retired. And while short selections from Literatures of the America text continue to be used, like other American curricula, much of University Lab School's curriculum focuses on British and American literature. Their experience illustrates the challenges and limitations of internationalizing literary curriculum in the most supportive of circumstances and suggests that other obstacles, such as a teacher training and a dearth of translations, stood in the way of internationalizing their curricula.

If cosmopolitanism requires a deep sense of the local, Bill's experience demonstrates how this rootedness must come *first*. Bill experienced his greatest success in drawing out student interest in international literature by connecting texts topically or thematically with students' lives. The school did this by comparing and contrasting student works with texts from North and South America, and through his lesson on the *Epic of Gilgamesh,* which connected the text to students' early experiences of death. While Bill did not describe any explicit intercultural dialogue as part of these lessons, an openness to the texts' narrative styles, characters, and worldviews are an inherent part of engaging cross-culturally. Bill's success with the *Epic of Gilgamesh* illustrates how teachers can foster engagement with international texts by making connections between texts and students' lived experiences.

Note

1. The term "local" gains additional resonance in the context of Hawai'i where "local" refers to long-time residents of Hawai'i, not necessarily of native Hawaiian ancestry. This terminology, which claims a sense of ownership and belonging, has been critiqued as a form of Asian settler colonialism (Fujikane & Okamura, 2008). Though perhaps not relevant to the discussion here, it is important to note this tension over the use of the term "local."

References

Chock, E., Harstad, J. R., Lum, D. H. Y., & Teter, B. (1998). *Growing up local: An anthology of poetry and prose from Hawai'i.* Honolulu, HI: Bamboo Ridge Press.

Damrosch, D. (2003). *What is world literature?* Princeton and Oxford: Princeton University Press.

Fujikane, C., & Okamura, J. Y. (2008). *Asian settler colonialism: From local governance to the habits of everyday life in Hawai'i.* Honolulu, HI: University of Hawai'i Press.

Harstad, J., & Harstad, C. (1981). *Asian-Pacific literature: Volumes I–III.* Hawai'i English Program Secondary-Management. State of Hawai'i Department of Education.

Lee, L., & Drick, G. (2001). *Literature of the Americas.* Honolulu, HI: Curriculum Research and Development Group.

Morikawa, K. (1994). The Home Court Advantage: Local Literature in Hawai'i's Schools. University of Hawai'i Honors Project. University of Hawai'i at Manoa.

Stanton, J. (1983). *British and European literatures: Volumes I–III.* Hawai'i English Program Secondary Management. State of Hawai'i Department of Education.

Teter, B. (2010). *Hapai na Leo.* Honolulu, HI: Curriculum Research and Development Group.

Chapter Four

Reading the *Bhagavad Gita* at a Buddhist School

Engendering Cosmopolitanism Through Shared Religious Ideas

While Bill succeeded in engaging students with the *Epic of Gilgamesh* by making connections to students' personal experiences, at Azabu Pacific[1], a small, Buddhist school, a shared school culture offered an opening to the sacred Hindu text the *Bhagavad Gita*.

While not all students and teachers at Azabu Pacific ascribed to a Buddhist philosophy, Buddhist values permeated the culture of the school. The only non-Japanese school in an association with five sister schools in Japan, Azabu Pacific is a small private school of about seventy-five students. As a college preparatory school that espouses Buddhist values, Azabu Pacific endeavors to "prepare students for college through academic excellence" but also to "enrich their lives with Buddhist values," and "develop their courage to nurture peace" (School Mission statement). As such, the school is guided by the six Buddhist virtues: selfless service, moral conduct, patience and perseverance, effort, contemplation, and wisdom. To this end, students take leadership roles in temple services helping out as the Master of Ceremony or lead chanter and providing aspirations—motivational quotes that are

Buddhist in nature. As a result of its Buddhist character, Azabu Pacific is known in the community as a "peace-based school."

Azabu's affiliations with its sister schools in Japan help to increase student contact with students from other countries from Japan and throughout Asia. Every year, two to five Azabu students travel to Japan to participate in the temple services and in cultural exchanges for one week. Select sophomores or juniors also have the opportunity to study abroad at sister schools, normally for six weeks but sometimes up to a full semester. Azabu Pacific, in turn, hosts several visiting Japanese students from these sister schools. In addition to these visiting Japanese students, Azabu's regular student body also includes foreign-born students from Korea, Mongolia, China and other areas, making Azabu Pacific a site of much transnational contact.

Despite its numerous international affiliations, Azabu Pacific's World Literature curriculum featured many canonical texts of the U.S. and British empires. While this suggests that the unique mission of the school did not influence curricular decisions, the funds of knowledge that circulated at the school did contribute to an openness among teachers and students to investigate different worldviews, evidenced in its unit on the *Bhagavad Gita*.

Tom

At the time that I met him, Tom had taught for three years and expressed an interest in international literature and education. Prior to teaching at Azabu, Tom had taught at an international school abroad, where he noted his curriculum was actually more western than his curriculum at Azabu. Tom did not consider himself an expert on Buddhism. However, he had become familiar with Buddhist teaching at the school and through his grandparents who he says "went to temple." To augment his knowledge of Buddhism and support the school mission, Tom sat in on courses in temple and Buddhist living offered at Azabu.

Having studied American literature in graduate school, Tom considered American literature his area of expertise and like many teachers, had no expertise in literary traditions outside the United States and Britain. He nevertheless expressed an interest and commitment to internationalizing curriculum. Originally suggested by an administrator with formal background on the text, the *Bhagavad Gita* was not a text Tom was familiar with. However, Tom expressed an openness to teaching the unfamiliar text and "put [his] own time into dissecting" it.

The *Bhagavad Gita*

One of the most important texts in Hindu tradition, the *Bhagavad Gita* comprises one book of the eighteen book *Mahabarata*, the sprawling epic poem seven times the length of the *Iliad* and the *Odyssey* combined. Composed between 200 B.C. and 200 A.D., the stories from the *Mahabarata* are portrayed in stone in Angkor Wat in Cambodia and in Indian paintings and continue to be written and told orally throughout South and Southeast Asia today.

In the *Bhagavad Gita*, the protagonist Arjuna goes into battle, and to his shock, encounters his own family members on the other side. He is faced with the ultimate ethical dilemma: should he follow his duty or his conscience? In contrast to many western texts, the god Krishna tells Arjuna he must fulfill his duty as a warrior without regard for the consequences—*he must kill his family*. Krishna gives this advice with the rationale that our physical manifestations are ephemeral.

So beloved is the *Bhagavad Gita*, the text has been translated more often and into more languages than any other Hindu text. Mahatma Ghandi is said to have turned to the *Gita* for daily inspiration in his struggle for India's independence. While the *Bhagavad Gita* is considered one of the most important texts of the Indian subcontinent and frequently included in high school anthologies of World Literature, the text's concepts, characters, and worldviews present unique pedagogical challenges for students and teachers unfamiliar with Hindu philosophy.

A Buddhist Reading of the *Bhagavad Gita*

In contrast to some teachers who have experienced great difficulty teaching the *Bhagavad Gita*, Tom counted his lesson on the *Bhagavad*

Gita as one of his most successful. Although Tom had never read the *Bhagavad Gita* before, an administrator with some familiarity of the text suggested it to Tom, and Tom took him up on the suggestion. With this "support system in place," Tom was "able to bounce ideas off him [the administrator]." From here, Tom researched the historical background of the text further and familiarized himself with concepts from the text.

"Not a conventional narrative," the two hundred-page excerpt of the edition that his class read did present challenges for Tom. As a spiritual Hindu text, the *Bhagavad Gita* shared concepts with Buddhism but was nevertheless philosophically different. As a result, lessons related to the concepts of dharma and rebirth confused his ninth graders. "Student confusion over rebirth was … an issue," Tom noted. Although the *Bhagavad Gita's* foreign narrative style proved challenging, it engaged students' critical thinking in a manner that forced them to confront cultural differences. Tom overcame these cultural and narrative differences by connecting it to the Buddhist principles of rebirth students at the school studied. Tom also engaged students by asking them to reflect on the broader themes of war and combat.

When the class read a scene, in which the god Krishna instructs the protagonist to kill his family, some students strongly disagreed or failed to understand. However, Tom used the scene as an opportunity to reflect on ethical dilemmas and different worldviews. Tom allowed his students to question the ancient text thereby engaging with the text by critiquing it. "Some of [the students] thought [Krishna] was arrogant. Some thought he had a lot of wisdom to speak. I just remember having a lot of debates about that," he said. In reading this foreign text, Tom allowed students to formulate their own responses to the characters; he did not force his students to adopt a particular view of Krishna, a pedagogical decision that encouraged students to formulate their own opinions about the lessons of the story.

Although the apparent lesson of the story of Krishna and Arjuna in the battlefield contradicted the ethos of the school, the text served as an entry point to discussions on how to avoid violence. "As a peace-based school," Tom said, "we had discussions about how that applies to things like actual armed combat or more metaphorical combats we have [like] conflicts in our daily lives." Tom connected the text to students' lives through the ongoing war in the Middle East. Tom extended the discussion to "metaphorical combat" or conflicts faced in our everyday life connecting the lesson to students' lives even further. Although individual students may not have had family members who served in the Middle East and may not have related to the theme of war, all students dealt with some "combat" or conflict in their life, Tom said. Tom took the text and used it as a jumping off place to connect it to students' lives.

Finally, Tom connected the Hindu story to Buddhist principles circulating at the school. "There was the idea of rebirth in that text," Tom said, "the idea of responsibility and accountability for your actions, motivations for your actions. The idea of rebirth, both in a literal and metaphorical sense." Although Hinduism presents a worldview distinct from Buddhism, with different mythological characters, values, and stories, Tom identified the theme of rebirth as a similarity between the two worldviews. "The confusion about what that means ['rebirth, both in a literal and metaphor sense'] was definitely something these students had," he admitted.

Rather than attempt to cover the text in a one-day lesson, Tom allowed several weeks for the unit, giving students an extended reading experience that allowed them to get to know the characters and adapt to the tone of the text. Reading the text over several weeks, Tom allowed students to inhabit the world of the text, giving students to space to ask lingering questions and air out their confusions.

Tom found that students did not agree with the moral of the story. Rather than shut down conversation, however, Tom allowed students to voice their discomfort and disagreement that allowed for deeper discussion. Students were forced to confront a world with values different from their own and ultimately to reconcile with those differences, one of the major characteristics of cosmopolitanism on the ground:

> A lot of times they want to be handed this easy digestible lesson. And have it feel good. … But sometimes they may have lingering doubts about it. Sometimes students will think about it and come back to class the next day and say *Wait a minute. What you were talking about? I don't get it.* Or *I don't agree with it.*
>
> [I was thinking] *Why is this guy still talking about that?* Just the lingering discussion with Krishna's point of view. … That's good fodder for debate.

Tom's students had difficulty agreeing with the moral of the story, but given the space to ask questions, the unfamiliar tropes and morals extended discussion rather than shutting it down. "Sometimes they just didn't agree with the lesson," Tom found, but given the space to disagree, he found, it was okay.

Tom admitted that the text was challenging for some students. When he read the text to his ninth graders, he found, only some of them understood. To address this problem, he had students work in groups with students who did understand, an activity that allowed advanced students to teach and sharpen their own understanding and allow students to teach one another. The text would have been too hard for English language learners (ELLs), he admitted:

> I think also there's nuances. It's not just a plot-based story. You're trying to take what's said and apply it in a spiritual cultural kind of way … that is difficult for them [ELLs] to do. They're more literal. … It would take some time to think beyond the plot reading of the book.

Although the vocabulary and translation may have appeared simple, the metaphorical nature of the stories made the text a difficult one, Tom admitted.

As an end of unit activity, Tom had students work in groups to recreate a scene from the text. "We try to do a modern day application of the *Bhagavad Gita*," Tom said where students can translate the events of the story into modern-day dialogue. "It was just trying to get them to … take the teachings in a relatable way." One group's project re-enacting a climactic chariot scene brought together a lot of their discussions. He counted this activity as one of his biggest successes in his World Literature course, he said.

> [The students' re-enactment] was nuanced. It wasn't something they pulled off of Spark Notes. It was something we had talked about in class. I watched the process unfold from point a to point b. So to see that on video was nice. … They were able to translate that into something that was relatable.

After the several-week long unit on a text many encountered difficulty with, students embraced the characters they may have disagreed with and acted them out, a move which demonstrated their understanding, if not their acceptance of the story.

Conclusion

Tom's facilitated a successful unit on the *Bhagavad Gita* in several ways. Although unfamiliar with the text, he augmented his own knowledge of the history, culture, and text with the help of an administrator at the school. He allowed his students to spend time with the text, enabling them to become comfortable with the pace, language, style, characters, and world of the text. He allowed students to ask questions. He paired students having difficulty with the text with stronger students. He engaged students through multimodal learning by having students re-enact the events of the text through dramatization. All of these pedagogical moves no doubt contributed to making his unit successful.

However, Tom's unit on the *Bhagavad Gita* proved challenging because it required students to reconcile what they knew with the foreign lessons of the text. As expected, students held on to their local allegiances but they also demonstrated an openness to the new. Many of the students in Tom's class rejected the lessons in the *Bhagavad Gita*. Their rejection of the text's lessons demonstrated a critical outlook while maintaining "loyalty to the known" (Hansen, 2010, p. 126). Students' wrangling with the text, thinking about the text even after the class had finished reading it, shows they were trying to assimilate it into their worldview. This wrangling demonstrates their understanding of the text's stylistic and cultural differences and a growing, if reluctant, openness. And Tom explained students had differing reactions to the text, some continuing to reject the text, others finding wisdom in it. Regardless of their response, students nevertheless immersed themselves in the Hindu text and engaged deeply with an outlook they may or may not have agreed with.

Tom helped to facilitate this critical outlook by allowing students to ask their questions and hesitations. He guided students toward an understanding of the text by connecting it to prior knowledge. He connected it to their lived experience further by pointing out the metaphorical implications of the text. While students may not have accepted the teaching of the *Bhagavad Gita*, they confronted the values and styles of another culture, came to an understanding of it, with an understanding they were allowed to question it.

Having been introduced to the concept of rebirth in their religion classes and in their weekly temple services, students meanwhile "wanted to understand rebirth" and the idea of karma. They had a vested interest in understanding the text. Familiarity with some of the concepts in the context of their Buddhist school offered an opening into the Hindu text.

Although Buddhism and Hinduism are vastly different worldviews, the Buddhist mission and culture helped contribute to an openness among faculty, administration, and students in understanding and coming to terms with the ancient, didactic text. The school mission, weekly temple rituals, visiting student body, and Buddhist course offerings all contributed to making school members more open to the unusual text.

Tom's unit on the *Bhagavad Gita* demonstrates how teachers can take a challenging foreign text and facilitate engagement by connecting it to student's prior knowledge and experiences. In this example, Tom's Buddhist students took an interest in the Buddhist idea of karma and rebirth, ideas all of the students in the school were familiar with through their regular temple services and the shared school culture. As a result of prior exposure to these ideas, Tom's students demonstrated an interest in better understanding these ideas. Like the students in my Catholic classroom who demonstrated a heightened interest in and knowledge of angels, Tom's students were engaged with something deeply familiar yet strangely different. As a result of their prior experience with the topics and themes, students had a vested interest in better understanding the text.

Note

1. In this chapter, the name of the school and teacher have been changed.

Reference

Hansen, D. T. (2010). Chasing butterflies without a net: Interpreting cosmopolitanism. *Studies in Philosophy and Education*, *29*(2), 151–166.

Chapter Five

Engaging Student Ethnic Identity at a Hawaiian School

Engendering Cosmopolitanism Through Culture-Based Values

"Begin at home. Then go out."

—Monica A. Ka'imipono Kaiwi

While Tom and Bill engaged their students with international literature by making connections to students' shared personal experiences or school cultures, Ka'imi, a teacher at a school for native Hawaiians, engaged students by rooting her curriculum in culture-based values. This meant including texts by native Hawaiians and that were about Hawai'i—a practice arguably antithetical to an internationalizing ethos. However, Ka'imi also opened up her curriculum and allowed her students to read a text from any part of the world by encouraging her students to read through a Hawaiian-values based lens. By connecting curriculum to ideas that were personal and relevant to them, Ka'imi engaged students with texts regardless of the text's provenance.

This chapter describes Ka'imi's unique school context and her journey in attempting to broaden her curriculum over thirty years. It describes the strategies and rubrics she and her department designed to engage her students with any text of the world—through Hawaiian culture-based values.

The unique context of Ka'imi's school played an important role in determining her curriculum. While Bill and Tom also taught in Hawai'i, Ka'imi taught at a school dedicated to native Hawaiians. Her school's unique demographic played an important role in determining the nature of the curriculum that engaged her students. A brief background is necessary to understand Kamehameha Schools, an important institution in the history of Hawai'i and of native Hawaiians.

Kamehameha Schools

Founded as a trust by Bernice Pauahi Bishop in 1887, Kamehameha School's mission per its trust is to educate the "children of Hawai'i" giving preference to pure or aboriginal blood (Pauahi's Will, 1883; as cited in Rohrer, 2010). As the great grand-daughter and last direct descendent of King Kamehameha I who united the Hawaiian islands (About Kamehameha Schools), Pauahi had witnessed the rapid decline of the Hawaiian population, language and culture, and in the final line item of her will, Pauahi, a childless heir, bequeathed the remainder of her fortune and real estate to establish Kamehameha Schools for the children of Hawai'i.

After statehood, land prices in Hawai'i increased and so did Kamehameha's trust. Currently boasting an endowment of $11 billion (Shimogawa, 2016), Kamehameha Schools is ranked among the most well-endowed schools in the United States. During the 1990s, Kamehameha boasted the largest endowment of any school, larger even than that of Harvard (Samuel & Roth, 2006). Since the 1990s, the trust's endowment dwindled. Nevertheless, Kamehameha Schools remains a large, powerful educational entity dedicated to educating Hawaiian youth. Today, Kamehameha Schools numerous campuses throughout the Hawaiian islands educate 5,000 to 6,000 pre-school to twelfth grade students (Rohrer, 2010), with 3,200 students at its flagship Kapālama campus where Ka'imi teaches (Kapālama Campus: K–12 Education, 2014).

Despite the school's dedication to servicing Hawaiian students, the school's curriculum has long espoused a Western-style pedagogy, a remnant of Hawai'i's missionary, colonial past. As late as the 1990s, the school hired only Protestants. When Ka'imi was hired 1989, she was the only Hawaiian member of the English department.

In 2002, Kamehameha administrators began talks of transforming Kamehameha from a school for Hawaiians to a "Hawaiian school." This vision of Kamehameha as a "Hawaiian school" became part of the official mission of the school with the new principal in 2006. By the time I interviewed Ka'imi in 2016, Kamehameha's policy of being a "Hawaiian school" had been in place for ten years.

According to the school website, 100% of 3,192 students on Ka'imi's campus are native Hawaiian. Despite the seemingly homogeneous nature of the student body, per the admissions policy, students come from all districts of Hawai'i. In addition, because of the historically high rate of intermarrying in Hawai'i, the student body is actually very ethnically diverse.

Ka'imi

In 1989, when Ka'imi arrived as a temporary hire, she was the only native Hawaiian in a department of thirty-two teachers, a replacement for another Hawaiian teacher out on sabbatical. Despite being Hawaiian,[1] having grown up in California, Ka'imi was nevertheless unfamiliar with Hawaiian traditions, values, and culture. "I didn't have any connection to here. ... I couldn't even pronounce my last name properly," she recalls.

Since those early days of teaching in Hawai'i, Ka'imi has grown personally as a Hawaiian and professionally as an educator and scholar. The story of her curriculums tells the story of her growth as a Hawaiian, of her department's struggle to broaden its curriculum, and her school's journey to become a Hawaiian school. In 2005, Ka'imi became the Department Chair of Kamehameha's English department, leading her department to broaden her department's curriculum and develop their own Hawaiian-based standards, used on several Kamehameha campuses throughout Hawai'i.

Leading the department and her school through curricular change was not easy, however. Despite the school's mission of educating Hawaiians, department members and administrators proved averse to incorporating culturally relevant pedagogy. Students, too, were sometimes uncomfortable with representations of Hawaiians in literature.

Culturally Relevant Pedagogy vs. Culture-Based Education

First theorized and elaborated upon by Gloria Ladson-Billings in 1995, culturally relevant pedagogy (CRP) connects school curriculum to students' culture by locating the "discontinuity between what they experience at home and what they experience at school" (p. 1). By connecting what students want to learn with what they need to learn (Ceppi, 2000), CRP asks curriculum developers to reflect on the sociocultural contexts of students' learning that connect school curriculum to students' identities (Moje, 2004). In this way, CRP is related to new literacy studies of students' out-of-school literacies (Gee, 2000) and pre-existing funds of knowledge (Clark, 2017; Moll, 1994). Like new literacy studies, which broaden educators' definition of literacy, CRP affirms the lives, experiences, and language of students.

While rooted in culturally relevant pedagogy, culture-based education (CBE), which Ka'imi's story demonstrates, presents curriculum relevant to students' cultures, not just their races or ethnicities. While CBE and CRP are both committed to centering students' lives, experiences, and backgrounds in the classroom curriculum and instruction, culture-based education differs from CRP in that it aims at instruction rooted in the values, norms, knowledge, beliefs, practices, experiences, places, and language of a cultural group (Kana'iaupuni, Ledward, & Malone, 2017). While culturally relevant pedagogy focuses primarily on racial and ethnic identity, culture-based education centers instruction around a culture, for example, Japanese, Jewish, Jesuit or Hawaiian culture. It differs from CRP in that aims to transmit and apply cultural ways of being, knowing, and doing (Kana'iaupuni et al., 2017). Like culturally relevant pedagogy, numerous studies have shown CBE to improve student academic success (Abt-Perkins & Rosen, 2000, Adams, Adams, & Opbroek, 2005; Kisker, et al., 2012; Lipka, Sharp, Brenner, Yanez, & Sharp, 2005; Rickard, 2005).

While Kana'iaupuni et al. (2017) distinguish culture-based education from culturally relevant pedagogy, seeing the two as part of a continuum of evolving approaches of culture in education, this book takes the view that culture-based education (CBE) and culturally relevant pedagogy are branches of the same tree and as such, part of the same family. Both CRP and CBE aim to present curriculum that is culturally relevant and affirm students' cultural identities.

Ka'imi's story illustrates one key difference between CBE and CRP. That is the cultural values component of CBE. The Hawaiian values embedded in some of Ka'imi's and her department's curriculum present strategies that stretch culturally relevant pedagogy by offering values-based curriculum unique to culture-based education. This paper illustrates two examples of culture-based educational strategies—Ka'imi's *makawalu* literary framework and her school's Hawaiian values based WEO anchor standards.

The Importance of Culturally Relevant Curriculum

Ka'imi realized early on in her teaching at Kamehameha that her students needed to connect with curriculum that was relevant to their experience, particularly as Hawaiians. The texts they were reading, texts including not just *Romeo and Juliet* but also multicultural texts such as *A Light in the Forest*, *The House on Mango Street*, and *The Joy Luck Club* were not related to their lived experience. As a result, students had difficulty engaging with them. She said, "They were like trees that were upside down, kind of trying to grasp, trying to connect in some way that was going to make sense." In this surreal image, Ka'imi envisioned her students as disconnected, uprooted and grasping at air rather than the soil they needed to survive. Over time, she began to see that "Hawaiian students were graduating from Kamehameha knowing all the literature of the world, except their own," a fact which spoke of the colonial mindset of Kamehameha and the state, which in Ka'imi's words was forever "enamored with things away."

Although as a recent transplant from Southern California with less familiarity with the Hawaiian references than her non-Hawaiian colleagues, she was open to learning and connecting students with curriculum that engaged them. When a senior colleague encouraged her to read *Waimea Summer*, Ka'imi took his advice. Set in Hawai'i and written by Hawaiian author John Dominis Holt, *Waimea Summer* evoked a world students were familiar with. Even though Ka'imi did not like the book or relate to it, she noticed that her students did:

> There was all this Hawaiian in there. I couldn't understand it ... and I didn't understand pidgin at all ... [but] it was really eye opening for me [because] my students got it ... they were actually connecting with it in a powerful way that they never had with the literature I was teaching.

The references in Hawaiian and to Hawai'i were foreign to Ka'imi, but the world was familiar to her students, and they appreciated and understood the book more than even she did. Although the text did not engage her personally, Ka'imi saw clearly it was working for her students. "I began to realize that by connecting it to Hawai'i, the kids were able to make connections and they knew more than I did," she said. The book's success in connecting with her students led her to keep the book on her syllabus and eventually, as she began to connect culturally with Hawai'i, Ka'imi gained a deeper understanding of the book.

Reading books like *Waimea Summer* in her classes was more than just an exercise in place-based pedagogy (Gruenewald, 2003a); reading literature set in Hawai'i served a political purpose and affirmed the legitimacy of her students' experience and identities:

> Now when they connect it to the literature from Hawai'i, they see themselves. They have a sense of identity. They see their place in the world as being something significant and they can actually contribute. But I think it empowers kids ... because they know where home is, and they're aware of the rest of the world.

Offering culturally relevant curriculum not only engaged students but gave them a sense of themselves in the world, a tenet of cosmopolitanism (Nussbaum, 1994; Todd, 2009).

Reading Texts Using Culturally Relevant Values

Ka'imi's work did not stop with culturally relevant texts. Over the years, she and her department developed a number of frameworks to promote culturally relevant values. The *makawalu* ("eight eyes") Literary Perspective framework, which she created in 2009 as an extension of her Master's degree, asks students to read texts using a Hawaiian epistemology. According to this framework, students are asked to consider texts based on characters' relationships to the *'āina* (land), *mo'okū'auhau* (genealogy or pedigree), *ho'omana* (spirituality), *ho'ailona* (signs or omens), and *ho'opono* (morality). Although each of the elements aligns with aspects of Western topics in literature, such as setting or character, each of the elements is deeply rooted in Hawaiian culture, including care for the land (*mālama 'āina*), the importance of family and lineage, a spiritual reverence for ancestors, the importance of a person's instinct or gut (*na'au*), and the importance of every person doing his or her part (*kūleana*).

This framework can be used for any text by any author, Hawaiian or non-Hawaiian. Reading *King Lear* by examining Lear's relationship to *'āina*, for example, reveals Lear's worldview and state of mind. "[When] he's in the storm and he's yelling about it ... [and] he's talking to nature," Ka'imi explained, his actions reveal a connection with the land and with nature, in keeping with Hawaiian values. When Lear gives up his power and hands it over to his daughters before he dies, his actions reveal his attitude toward his *mo'okū'auhau* (genealogy). In rejecting tradition and even his royal lineage, Lear "pretty much

Table 5.1: Makawalu Literary Perspectives (Excerpt).

Elements of Hawaiian World View	English Translation*	Aspects of Hawaiian Perspective in Literature	Aspects of Western Perspective in Literature
'āina	Land, earth	Familial, genealogical relationship with āina through hāloa; kūleana (responsibility) includes mālama o ka 'āina (caring for the land); aloha 'āina (love of the land); *kaona*	Mother Nature; objective human/environment relationship; Man vs. Nature; untamed Wilderness; living off the land; getting back to nature; personification, imagery, allegory, metaphor, setting, simile
mo'okū'auhau	Genealogical succession; pedigree	Status determined by genealogy—ancestors, parents, children, *kumu*; *kaona*	Status determined by position/job–wealth; connections; respect; point-of-view, protagonist, antagonist, characterization

Source: *Pukui, Mary Kawena and Samuel H. Elbert. *Hawaiian Dictionary*. Honolulu: University of Hawai'i Press, 1986.

breaks traditions, and breaks the *mo'okū'auhau*. So what happens? It backfires," Ka'imi said. Just as students might read a text with a feminist framework or a Marxist framework, using the Makawalu Literary Perspectives, students grapple with texts using a Hawaiian framework with Hawaiian values as guiding principles.

In another lesson, students compare and contrast Jack London's *Ko'olau the Leper* to a version of the same story entitled *Kaluaioko'olau* written by Ko'olau's wife Pi'ilani. In both books, the authors tell the harrowing tale of a leper who successfully evaded capture by the authorities by hiding out for years in the remote valley of Kalalau on Kaua'i's rugged northern coast.

Whereas London's description of Kalalau valley revealed it to be "wild and dangerous and in opposition to you," in Pi'ilani's version, the valley was "this comforting place." For Pi'ilani, the valley "is *'ohana* (family)." The two renderings of the same tale offer different interpretations that reveal the subjectivity of the author. Using the *makuwalu* framework, Ka'imi allows her students to use Hawaiian values as an entry point into discussions of diction and differing worldviews. These lessons articulate and clarify Hawaiian values and help to situate those values in texts from around the world, not just about their own culture.

Grappling with Students' Hawaiian Identities: Encountering Student Resistance

Through encounters with culturally relevant texts of and about Hawaiians, students sometimes encountered content that challenged their identity as Hawaiians. Generations of students at Kamehameha, for example, have grappled with the fact of Hawaiian polytheism, and students sometimes blamed Ka'imi when their reading list included unflattering representations of Hawaiians. In investigating Hawaiian spirituality, Christian students sometimes had difficulty reconciling Hawai'i's four-thousand akua (god or element) with their own contemporary religious worldview. "Can you be Hawaiian and still be a Christian?" Ka'imi asked her classes. During the 1990s, she saw that one or two students in each class "really, really struggled with it." "My students thought it was heathen," she recalls. Over the past thirty years, Ka'imi has noticed that these attitudes have dissipated. Students no longer grapple with Hawaiian literature as heathenism, a fact that Ka'imi said shows "we're evolving." Through these encounters with the self, students invariably encountered a different worldview and were forced to recognize "the other" within even their own culture.

Student disapproval of their own culture came in different contexts. In one text *Voyaging Chiefs of Havai'i* by Teuira Henry and others, one of the characters beat and killed his wife. Enraged at being exposed to unflattering images of her ancestors, one student wrote a letter challenging Ka'imi. "'How dare you destroy my perception of my ancestors!'" Ka'imi recalled the letter reading. Like the students who grappled with the reality of their polytheist ancestors, this student had difficulty accepting that a chief of Polynesia would beat his wife and that his or her teacher would expose students to this representation of Pacific Islanders. Students did not need to go outside their culture to encounter differing worldviews. In fact, the differing worldviews with the people closest to them proved to be the most impactful and difficult to reconcile.

Ka'imi justified the inclusion of these negative representations of Hawaiians in her curriculum with the belief that idealizing the past was not in her students' best interest. "They need to see the good and the bad ... Their *mo'okū'auhau* have people who made mistakes. We can learn from them. And we can move forward," she said. Reading culturally relevant texts gave students an opportunity to solidify and articulate their own worldviews, not only those related to non-Hawaiians, but to Hawaiians who were also different from them. Culturally relevant texts challenged their perceptions of their ancestors and themselves, engaged students with issues that were deeply personal and relevant, and forced them to articulate their worldviews.

Perhaps the most remarkable example of students grappling with representations of self came in their reading of Herman Melville's *Typee*. Though Melville was a sojourner through Hawai'i, his work was long recognized as representing the literature of the Pacific, a problematic categorization that confirmed colonial attitudes about Hawai'i. It confirmed that Caucasian outsiders passing through Hawai'i should be allowed to speak authoritatively on behalf of Pacific Islanders, that

Hawaiians could not write literature, and that Hawaiian cultural productions were not valuable. This problematic practice of teaching the writing of sojourners as Literature of the Pacific continued at the University of Hawai'i well into the 1990s, but has been widely critiqued since (personal correspondence, Morales, 2015).

Despite the politics surrounding the text, Ka'imi embraces *Typee* as a way to engage students' higher order thinking skills. "I choose to teach [*Typee*]," Ka'imi explained, "because I think it's important. If you don't like something, you can't complain unless you read the whole thing. … It gives me the right to voice my opinion when I've endured it all." She uses the text to draw out student responses to overtly racist commentary by an author widely regarded as one of America's greatest. In the book, Melville calls King Kamehameha III a "negro-looking blockhead" and a "dram drunk" while the text describes Queen Ka'ahumanu "a monstrous Jezebel." "He was not as sympathetic to natives as most of his scholars would say," Ka'imi explained. "He was right in line with his contemporaries. He was racist." Not only did Melville reflect the racist views of his time, but by writing about it, he further circulated and perpetuated these negative views. "[But] the book still exists so what do we do with the book?" Ka'imi asks her students. Forced to reconcile outsiders' views of Hawaiians, students are given permission to engage with a text without necessarily liking it. "That becomes part of their analysis," she said.

Despite the challenges associated with some aspects of Ka'imi's curriculum, the effectiveness of Ka'imi's Hawaiian values-based curriculum is evidenced in the students and parents who have thanked Ka'imi for her work over the years. When the Assistant Head of School saw that her son was liking English for the first time as a result of Ka'imi's Hawaiian values-based curriculum, she approached Ka'imi and told her, "You need to share this with everybody … In all these years, my son has never connected with literature and now that he sees this, he is now excited about it."

Former students continue to come back to her to express their appreciation and tell Ka'imi how her approaches helped them in their post-secondary studies. One student even discussed Ka'imi's framework as a model for her Master's thesis, for which the student won an award. In short, despite the challenges of broaching uncomfortable identity issues, Ka'imi's culturally relevant curriculum and pedagogy engaged students deeply and prepared them for their future studies.

Hawaiian Values-Based Standards

In the early 2000s, school members on all three of Kamehameha's campuses together drafted the Working Exit Outcomes (WEO),[2] articulating the school's expectations for its graduates. Reflecting the school's interest in transforming into a "Hawaiian school," Kamehameha's WEOs include "Embrace my identity as a Hawaiian," "Promote and utilize Hawaiians' perspectives," "Engage in critical thinking to apply traditional knowledge to my contemporary context," and "Live in interdependence with all that surrounds me physically, spiritually, emotionally, and intellectually." These Working Exit Outcomes were written to reflect Hawaiian values in keeping with the school's interest in becoming a Hawaiian school.

Divided into three broad categories—Identity, Seek and Apply Knowledge, and Communicate, the six-page WEO ELA standards reflect an inward to outward looking continuum. The standards ask students to reflect on their identity in the context of their setting, ancestry, and the world (Identity). It asks students to interact with sources and create original work (Seek and Apply Knowledge). Finally, it asks students to communicate their ideas in a variety of mediums and formats and for different audiences and purposes (Communicate).

While superficially similar to other ELA standards, the inclusion of Hawaiian values such as *mo'okuauhau* (genealogy), *kūleana* (purpose and place), and *mo'olelo* (story) distinguish Kamehameha's standards from other standards. By integrating Hawaiian ideas and ways of knowing, school leaders call upon teachers and students to understand and reflect on these Hawaiian values. For example, while students reflect on setting, a common component of language arts curriculum, when appropriate, students and teachers are also called on to reflect on *wahi pana* (legendary place), *hānau* (birth place), and *ahupua'a*, the ancient mountain-to-ocean land divisions which promoted sustainable land management. In seeking and applying knowledge, students and teachers discuss *kūleana*, the term referring not only to purpose and place but also to a sense of privilege and jurisdiction. Teachers ask students to understand texts with the underlying belief that this study is rooted in students' purpose and position in life. In communicating their knowledge, the WEO standards remind teachers and students to "adapt successfully to various *kūlana*," in other words to practice humility appropriately. By including Hawaiian language and values, these standards articulate and highlight key Hawaiian values, honor culturally relevant values and ways of knowing, declare a commitment to Hawaiian values, and make a promise to try to incorporate these values into the English curriculum.

Table 5.2: Working Exit Outcome (WEO) English Language Arts (ELA) Anchor Standards (Excerpt).

Identity		
WEO Connections	**ELA/WEO Anchors**	**Embedded Hawaiian Epistemology/Nohona**
• WEO: "Embrace my identity as a Hawaiian" • WEO: "Nurture and value my identity as source of understanding, purpose, meaning and connection to others." • WEO: "Engage in critical thinking to apply traditional knowledge to contemporary context."	**ID2.GR 9/10:** Students will be able to independently articulate how mo'okūauhau shapes/influences identity, both in self and in text (e.g., spiritually, socially, intellectually, historically, biologically). **ID2.GR 11/12:** Students will be able to independently analyze how mo'okūauhau (genealogy) impacts character development in works of literature (e.g., Texts, film).	**ID2:** Reflects an understanding that mo'okū'auhau specifies one's "family members and their connection to the source" (Kanahele, 4) and it is through these connections that mana and social standing is established (Campbell). This WEO Anchor applies a similar perspective by analyzing a character's relationship with or lack of relationship with 'ohana as an additional means by which to examine character development.

Source: Working Exit Outcome (WEO) English Language Arts (ELA).

Discussion

Ka'imi's project went beyond expanding the canon to include texts by Hawaiians and about Hawai'i. Through her *makawalu* framework and WEO ELA anchor standards, Kamehameha's pedagogy took up culturally relevant frameworks that allowed her students to read any text in a culturally relevant manner—with an attention to students' cultural values and histories. By providing a lens for students to see Hawaiian values and ways of knowing in any literature, it helped make any literature relevant to her native Hawaiian students in her class. A values-based, culture-based curriculum opened up the possibilities of culturally relevant pedagogy.

It should be noted that Kamehameha's Hawaiian values-based curriculum and standards required *articulating* the values of the Hawaiian culture, an effort which drew from existing scholarship on Hawaiian epistemology and Hawaiian creation stories, and a commitment to pursuing culturally relevant curriculum as Ka'imi demonstrated through her graduate research. Implementing a culturally relevant values-based curriculum required significant resources and manpower, including the efforts of individuals at the school level and in academia with a shared vision of what it meant to be Hawaiian.

While Ka'imi's curriculum illustrates a values-based curriculum that distinguishes it from most culturally relevant pedagogy, this values-based curriculum is only achievable with the articulation of a culture's shared values, which was made possible in this case by Ka'imi and others at Kamehameha and by an existing pantheon of Hawaiian texts from which to draw its values.

Cosmopolitanism on the Ground

Like much cosmopolitan theory, which maintains an appreciation for the Other must stem from our local experiences, Ka'imi's curriculum demonstrated cosmopolitanism by encouraging both rootedness and a critical attitude toward others and the self. While Ka'imi took great interest in exposing students to curriculum relevant to their place and their history, her pedagogical goals also had to do with students understanding their place in the world and thereby connecting with the larger world.

When she envisioned her students as upside trees disconnected from what they needed to orient themselves, she offers a startling image of Appiah's "rooted cosmopolitanism" gone awry. Unable to connect to either the canonical or multicultural texts in their curriculum because it had little connection with their own experience, students had difficult engaging in the curriculum. It was only through a sense of rootedness and belonging that students were able to engage with texts about experiences different than their own. Her example demonstrates what numerous cosmopolitan theorists have conjectured (Appiah, 1997, Forte, Roberts, Murray, & Gray, 2002; Hansen, 2009; Hansen, 2010a; Hansen, 2010b; Koh, 2008; Lingard, Nixon, & Ransom, 2008, Nussbaum, 1994; Rizvi, 2014; Rizvi & Beech, 2017; Sobe, 2008; Sobe & Kowalczyk, 2012; Werbner, 2008), that cosmopolitanism must be expressed in context. Ka'imi's curriculum appreciated the importance of local socialization (Hansen, 2010b).

The idea of orientating students so "they're aware of the rest of the world" also spoke to the Hawaiian value of kūleana, included in both the Makawalu "eight eyes" literary framework the WEO anchor standards. Kūleana, the Hawaiian word denoting purpose, jurisdiction, duty, and calling, itself spoke to the idea of cosmopolitanism, which asks students to consider their relationship with the wider world. Ka'imi's Hawaiian values based curriculum explicitly asked students to consider their purpose vis-à-vis the text and themselves. The cosmopolitan idea of connection to the world were embedded in her curriculum through its Hawaiian values.

While Ka'imi grounded her curriculum in the local, her curriculum very much allowed students to demonstrate a critical attitude toward both the known and the new, one of the distinguishing characteristics of cosmopolitanism on the ground (Hanson, 2010b). When students faced unflattering images of native Hawaiians depicted by Hawaiians and non-Hawaiians alike, these texts challenged students' worldviews. Students were forced to grapple with and reconcile their worldviews to the texts.' Students in Ka'imi's class were forced to demonstrate Hansen's "receptivity to the new" and "loyalty to the known" (2006, p. 126).

They had no choice but to make sense of these differing worldviews, because their identities were implicated in the curriculum.

One might argue that reading through a "local lens" does not demonstrate the "reflective openness" of cosmopolitanism. Rather, it imposes readers' understandings and values onto another culture.

I would argue that it is difficult to read cross culturally without reading through one's own cultural lens. In Ka'imi's example, articulating those values helped clarify and magnify those values so as to make them explicit. Ka'imi's students did not come to the text without the assumption that Hawaiian values were the only values. Rather, the cross-cultural reading affirmed an understanding of their culture as it applied in another context. This recognition of one's cultural uniqueness has been described as one aspect of cosmopolitanism (Hansen, 2010b).

Limitations

The example of Kamehameha Schools is unique and difficult to replicate. Because of its unique mission, Kamehameha is able to teach to a specific ethnic group. The school's racial homogeneity may also allow for sensitive discussions on race and culture that would be highly charged in the ethnically heterogeneous classrooms that characterize many classrooms. Whereas teachers who incorporate culturally relevant curriculum can risk singling out minority students (Dudley-Marling, 2003; Gaudelli, 2003), Ka'imi and the teachers in her department did not have to deal with such issues. In short, Kamehameha had the luxury of a racially homogenous classroom, which few schools can replicate.

Nevertheless, it should be noted Kamehameha is also racially diverse. While Kamehameha's admissions policy suggests that 100% of the students are of Hawaiian ancestry, in fact, due to the intermarrying that has occurred since Western contact and Kamehameha's acceptance of increasingly smaller percentages of Hawaiian blood, Kamehameha's student body is incredibly diverse, including students from many different ethnicities. Even individuals who are ethnically Hawaiian may not be perceived and accepted as Hawaiian (Ledward, 2007; Reelitz,

2013), and students may identify as Hawaiian to differing degrees. In choosing to attend the school, however, both students and teachers commit to a certain extent to learning about Hawaiian culture, now an overt mission of the school.

Conclusion

According to Ka'imi, prior to the expansion of Kamehameha's curriculum under her leadership, her students had been weaned on a diet of colonial curriculum, which did not speak to their lived experienced as Hawaiians. Rather, they needed to learn about their Hawaiian culture and history. Without this sustaining knowledge rooted in Hawaiian values and texts, Ka'imi's students were upside down, taking in air when they needed to be grounded and rooted in their culture. According to her metaphor, given a colonial curriculum, her students were slowly dying. The texts forced difficult discussions, which engaged students, had students coming back to her for years even after they had graduated. Fiercely decolonizing in its values and outlook, using a framework based on Hawaiian values, Ka'imi curriculum engaged her students with any literature of the world by rooting it in the culture and values that were personally relevant to them. Ka'imi's curriculum demonstrates how teachers can make connections not only through content that is topically relevant to students' ethnic identities. Her curriculum demonstrates reading strategies that highlight culture-based values that can be applied to any text.[3]

Notes

1. Ka'imi is ethnically Hawaiian and Russian.
2. WEO means "the dawning," a name intentionally chosen to mark the dawning of a new era at Kamehameha.
3. As of the writing of this chapter, the WEO standards, developed with input from all three of Kamehameha's campuses, are no longer used at Kamehameha's Maui and Big Island campuses. It is currently used only by Kamehameha's Oahu campus, where Ka'imi remains English Department Chair.

References

About Kamehameha Schools. (1996–2016). Kamehameha schools. Retrieved in 2016 from http://www.ksbe.edu/about_us/about_kamehameha_schools/

Abt-Perkins, D., & Rosen, L. (2000). Preparing English teachers to teach diverse student populations: Beliefs, challenges, proposals for change. *English Education, 32*(4), 251–266.

Achinstein, B., & Ogawa, R. T. (2012). New teachers of color and culturally responsive teaching in an era of educational accountability: Caught in a double bind. *Journal of Educational Change, 13*(1), 1–39.

Adams, B., Adams, S., & Opbroek, M. (2005). Reversing the academic trend for rural students: The case of Michelle Opbroek. *Journal of American Education, 44*(3), 55–79.

Appiah, A. (1997). Cosmopolitan patriots. *Critical Inquiry, 23*(3), 617–639.

Bell, Y. R., & Clark, T. R. (1998). Culturally relevant reading material as related to comprehension and recall in African American children. *Journal of Black Psychology, 24*(4), 455–475.

Ceppi, A. (2000). *Examining a culturally relevant, community based secondary education program: The Wai'anae High School Hawaiian Studies Program.*

Clark, K. (2017). Investigating the effects of culturally relevant texts on African American struggling readers' progress. *Teachers College Record, 119*(5), 1–30.

Dudley-Marling, C. (2003). "I'm not from Pakistan": Multicultural literature and the problem of representation. In D. Fox & K. Short (Eds.), *Stories matter: The complexity of cultural authenticity in children's literature* (pp. 3–24). Urbana, IL: National Council of Teachers of English.

Forte, M., Roberts, M., Murray, D., & Gray, J., & Dept. of Anthropology. (2002). *Re-engineering indigeneity: Cultural brokerage, the political economy of tradition, and the Santa Rosa Carib Community of Arima, Trinidad & Tobago* (Doctoral Dissertation). National Library of Australia.

Gaudelli, W. (2003). *World class: Teaching and learning in global times.* Mahwah, NJ: L. Erlbaum Associates.

Gee, J. P. (2000). New people in new worlds: Networks, the new capitalism and schools. In B. Cope & M. Kalantzis (Eds.), *Multiliteracies: Literacy learning and the design of social futures* (pp. 43–68). London & New York: Routledge.

Grant, C. A. (1973). Black studies materials do make a difference. *The Journal of Educational Research, 66*(9), 400–404.

Gruenewald, D. A. (2003a). Foundations of place: A multidisciplinary framework for place-conscious education. *American Educational Research Journal, 40*(3), 619–654.

Gruenewald, D. A. (2003b). The best of both worlds: A critical pedagogy of place. *Educational Researcher, 32*(4), 3–12.

Hansen, D. T. (2009). Dewey and cosmopolitanism. *Education and Culture, 25*(2).

Hansen, D. T. (2010a). Chasing butterflies without a net: Interpreting cosmopolitanism. *Studies in Philosophy and Education, 29*(2), 151–166.

Hansen, D. T. (2010b). Cosmopolitanism and education: A view from the ground. *Teachers College Record, 112*(1), 1–30.

Kaiwi, M. K. (2006). Grounding Hawaiian learners—and teachers—in their indigenous identity. *Hulili, 3*(1), 27–36.

Kaiwi, M. K., & Kahumoku, W. III (2006). Makawalu: Standards, curriculum, and assessment for literature through an indigeno us perspective. *Hulili, 3*(1), 183–206.

Kaiwi, M. K. (2007). *Typee*: Melville's "contribution" to the well-being of native Hawaiians. In J. Barnum, W. Kelly, & C. Sten (Eds.). *"Whole oceans away": Melville and the Pacific* (pp. 3–16). Kent, OH: Kent State University Press.

Kana'iaupuni, S. M., Ledward, B., & Malone, N. (2017). Mohala i ka wai: Cultural advantage as a framework for indigenous culture-based education and student outcomes. *American Educational Research Journal, 54*(1), 311S–339S.

Kisker, E., Lipka, J., Adams, B., Rickard, A., Andrew-Ihrke, D., Yanez, E., & Millard, A. (2012). The potential of a culturally based supplemental mathematics curriculum to improve the mathematics performance of Alaska Native and other students. *Journal for Research in Mathematics Education, 43*(1), 75–113.

Koh, A. (2008). Deparochializing education: Re-envisioning education in ASEAN. In B. Lingard, J. Nixon, & S. Ranson (Eds.), *Transforming learning in schools and communities: The remaking of education for a cosmopolitan society* (pp. 37–49). New York & London: Continuum Books.

Ladson-Billings, G. (1995). But that's just good teaching! The case for culturally relevant pedagogy. *Theory Into Practice, 34*(3), 159–165.

Ledward, B. (2007). On being Hawaiian enough: Contesting American racialization with native hybridity. *Hulili, 4*(1), 107–143.

Lingard, B., Nixon, J., & Ranson, S. (2008). Remaking education for a globalized world: Policy and pedagogic possibilities. In B. Lingard, J. Nixon, and S. Ranson (Eds.), *Transforming learning in schools and communities: The remaking of education for a cosmopolitan society* (pp. 3–36). New York & London: Continuum Books.

Lipka, J., Sharp, N., Brenner, B., Yanez, E., & Sharp, F. (2005). The relevance of culturally based curriculum and instruction: The case of Nancy Sharp. *Journal of American IndianEducation, 44*(3), 31–54.

Meyers, M. A. (2001). Our own liberation: Reflections on Hawaiian epistemology. *The Contemporary Pacific, 13*(1), 124–148.

Moje, E. J. (2004). Powerful spaces: Tracing the out-of-school literacy spaces of Latino/a youth. In K. Leander & M. Sheehy (Eds.), *Spatializing literacy research and practice*, (pp. 15–38). New York, NY: Peter Lang.

Moll, L. C. (1994). Mediating knowledge between homes and classrooms. In D. Keller-Cohen (Ed.), *Literacy: Interdisciplinary conversations* (pp. 385–410). Cresskill, NJ: Hampton Press.

Nussbaum, M. (1994). Patriotism and cosmopolitanism. *Boston Review*. Retrieved from http://bostonreview.net/martha-nussbaum-patriotism-and-cosmopolitanism

Pauahi's W. (1883). Kamehameha schools. Retrieved in 2016 from http://www.ksbe.edu/about_us/about_pauahi/will/

Pukui, M. K., & Elbert, S. H. (1986). *Hawaiian dictionary*. Honolulu, HI: University of Hawai'i Press.

Reelitz, K. (2013, Sept./Oct). Hawaiian enough: Transforming Hawaiian identities. *Hana Magazine*. pp. 2633.

Rickard, A. (2005). Constant perimeter, varying area: A case study of teaching and learning mathematics to design a fish rack. *Journal of American Indian Education, 44*(3), 80–100.

Rizvi, F. (2014). *Encountering Education in the Global*. London & New York: Routledge.

Rizvi, F. & Beech, J. (2017). Global mobilities and the possibilities of a cosmopolitan curriculum. *Curriculum Inquiry, 47*(1), 125–134.

Rohrer, J. (2010). Attacking trust: Hawai'i as a crossroads and Kamehameha Schools in the crosshairs. *American Quarterly, 62*(3), 437–455.

Samuel, K., & Roth, R. (2006). *Broken trust: Greed, mismanagement, and political manipulation at America's largest charitable trust*. Honolulu, HI: University of Hawai'i Press.

Shimogawa, D. (2016, January 6). Kamehameha schools endowment reaches $11.1B, annual report says. *Pacific Business News*. Retrieved in 2016 from http://www.bizjournals.com/pacific/news/2016/01/05/kamehameha-schools-endowment-reaches-11-1b-annual.html

Sobe, W. N. (2008). *Provincializing the worldly citizen: Yugoslav student and teacher travel and Slavic cosmopolitanism in the internet era*. New York, NY: Peter Lang.

Sobe, N. & Kowalczyk, J. (2012). The problem of context in comparative education research. *Educational, Cultural and Psychological Studies, 3*(6), 55–74.

Todd, S. (2009). *Toward an imperfect education: Facing humanity, rethinking cosmopolitanism*. Boulder, CO: Paradigm.

Werbner, P. (Ed.). (2008). *Anthropolgy and the new cosmopolitanism: Rooted, feminist, and vernacular perspectives*. Oxford, UK: Berg.

Literary Works Cited

Cisneros, Sandra. (1984.) *The House on Mango Street*.

Henry, Teuira. (1974). *Voyaging Chiefs of Havai'i*.

Holt, John Dominis. (1995). *Waimea Summer*.

London, Jack. (1919). "Koolau the Leper." *The House of Pride, and Other Tales of Hawaii* (pp. 47–91).

Melville, Herman. (1846). *Typee*.

Pi'ilani. (1906). *Kaluaioko'olau*.

Richter, Conrad. (1953). *The Light in the Forest*.

Shakespeare, William. (1597). *Romeo and Juliet*.

Shakespeare, William. (1623). *The Tempest*.

Tan, Amy. (1989). *The Joy Luck Club*.

Chapter Six

Conclusion

Together these teachers' stories illustrate the power of connecting international curriculum to students' lives. Ka'imi did this through connections to Hawaiian values and culture, important to many of the students at Kamehameha. Tom did this by connecting Buddhist principles to Hindu ideas. Bill did this by making connections to students' personal experiences of death.

Their students' experiences are similar to those described by cosmopolitan theorists Sobe and Forte who describe groups finding affinities transnationally. The Slavs and indigenous individuals Sobe and Forte describe, for example, identified with Slavs and indigenous individuals in other countries and came to a richer awareness of their culture and themselves. This connection is similar to the connections forged in Bill and Tom's classes where shared personal experiences and familiar religious principles helped engender connections cross culturally. Ka'imi's curriculum is different. Proudly situating the culture-based values at the forefront of the cross cultural reading, this curriculum emphasized cultural difference and uniqueness.

A recognition of sameness and difference were inherent in all the teachers' experiences, however. Even Ka'imi's culture-based readings likely involved the realization that the Hawaiian connection to land and lineage was also important in Renaissance England. While the *Bhagavad Gita* hooked Buddhist students in with familiar concepts, making meaning of the text involved a confrontation with cultural difference and a reconciliation of students' prior understanding of karma and rebirth. Reading cross culturally involves reading for both difference and sameness, an observation that has been made many times before (Boglatz, 2005; Cooppan, 2009; Koh, 2008; Nikola-Lisa, 2003; Short, 2012; Spivak & Mohanty, as cited in Needham, 2009; Thomas, 2007). These teachers' experiences illustrate how both sameness and difference can be used as entrees into international literature. While usually readers make connections by identifying similarities, Ka'imi's example suggests that fore-fronting difference can provide another strategy to engage students with reading cross culturally.

Finding international texts that relate to our students' experiences is not simply about universal themes, however. It's about finding the universal themes that matter to our particular students. A story about karma and rebirth might not have engaged students at a Catholic school. And the connections to land and family, so important at Ka'imi's school, may not have engaged the students at Tom's school in the same way it did in Ka'imi's classroom. Finding universal themes is a start, but engaging students—particularly when reading cross culturally—means finding universal themes that connect with the specific lived experiences of the students in our class.

In this book, the term "local" has referred to students' specific experiences vis-à-vis their ethnic identity, personal experiences, and religious affiliations. This is in keeping with cosmopolitan theorists who have used the term "local" in association with the individual (Biesta & Laury, as cited in Rizvi & Beech, 2017); place (Forte, Roberts, Murray, & Gray, 2002, Werbner, 2008); and enacted experience (Appiah, 1998; Forte et al., 2002; Gough, 2000; Werbner, 2008). While the local is multisited (Forte et al., 2002) and emblems of a particular affiliation can move around and gain new life, these teachers' experiences suggest that cosmopolitanism on the ground must begin with our students' parochial identities. Only by making connections to students' localized experiences can we hope to engender connections to others places and cultures.

References

Appiah, K. W. (1998). Cosmopolitan patriots. In P. Cheah & B. Robbins (Eds.), *Cosmopolitics: Thinking and feeling beyond the nation* (pp. 91–116). Minneapolis, MN: University of Minnesota Press.

Boglatz, J. (2005). *Talking race in the classroom.* New York, NY: Teachers College Press.

Cooppan, V. (2009). The ethics of world literature: Reading others, reading otherwise. In D. Damrosch (Ed.), *Teaching world literature* (pp. 34–43). New York, NY: The Modern Language Association of America.

Forte, M., Roberts, M., Murray, D., Gray, J., & Dept. of Anthropology. (2002). *Re-engineering indigeneity: Cultural brokerage, the political economy of tradition, and the Santa Rosa Carib Community of Arima, Trinidad & Tobago* (Doctoral Dissertation). National Library of Australia.

Gough, N. (2000). Locating curriculum studies in the global village. *Journal of Curriculum Studies, 32*(2), 329–42.

Koh, A. (2008). Deparochializing education: Re-envisioning education in ASEAN. In B. Lingard, J. Nixon, & S. Ranson (Eds.), *Transforming learning in schools and communities: The remaking of education for a cosmopolitan society* (pp. 37–49). New York & London: Continuum Books.

Needham, A. D. (2009). The place of difference in cross-cultural literacy. In D. Damrosch (Ed.), *Teaching World Literature* (pp. 73–85). New York, NY: The Modern Language Association of America.

Nikola-Lisa, W. (2003). "Around my table" is not always enough. In D. Fox & K. Short (Eds.), *Stories matter: The complexity of cultural authenticity in children's literature* (pp. 46–49). Urbana, IL: National Council of Teachers of English.

Rizvi, F., & Beech, J. (2017). Global mobilities and the possibilities of a cosmopolitan curriculum. *Curriculum Inquiry, 47*(1), 125–134.

Short, K. G. (2012). Story as world making. *Language Arts, 90*(1), 9–17.

Thomas, L. (2007). When literature discussion seems to go nowhere: Reevaluating teaching and learning. *WOW Stories: Connections from the Classrooms, 1*(1). Retrieved from http://wowlit.org/on-line-publications/

Werbner, P. (Ed.). (2008). *Anthropology and the new cosmopolitanism: Rooted, feminist, and vernacular perspectives.* Oxford, UK: Berg.

Chapter Seven

Modern Chinese Literature Curriculum

WITH YUN PENG

Trying to anticipate which topics or themes will connect with our students requires a certain amount of clairvoyance. It requires knowing the students in our classrooms. And it requires trial and error. One teacher I spoke with shared how the students in her inner city school in Los Angeles very much engaged with William Goldings' *Lord of the Flies*, because the story was ultimately about gangs, which many of her students understood. This teacher understood that *Lord of the Flies* was about gangs, but she had not foreseen the extent to which students would relate.

Because we cannot know your classroom contexts, it is difficult to make specific suggestions for individual classroom teachers trying to connect international literature selections with students. This is the job of individual teachers who know what will work with their students far better than any standardized curriculum.

That said, given the dearth of international literature curriculum and the need for more teacher resources, we offer here a few suggestions of modern Chinese literature. The stories highlighted have been selected for their literary merit, for their accessibility to the average high school student, and for the inclusion of themes developmentally relevant for many teens.

Why China?

Known as the "Middle Kingdom" or center of the world for millennia, China was for many years the dominant power in Asia. China maintained vassal states throughout Asia, including regions known today at Vietnam and Korea. In deference to the powerful Middle Kingdom, these vassal states gave considerable wealth in the form of pottery and other goods that satiated imperial powers for generations. So powerful was China by the late-1400s, it had all the tools it needed to colonize the world including water-tight ships, navigating instruments, and gunpowder. Rather than take over the world, however, China remained content with its holdings.

In the centuries that followed, European countries such as Spain, Portugal, France, Belgium, Britain, and others traveled to and colonized Africa, the Americas, and even China. (The British held Hong Kong from 1841 to 1997.) The question of why China did not colonize the rest of the world remains an enduring question in history.

Today, China remains one of the largest and most important nations of the world. Constituting roughly 1/7 of the world population, China is where many of the world's products come from. It is also where much of the world's recycling waste ends up. And perhaps most importantly for language arts teachers, China has a long literary history made possible by its scholarly and literate class.

In an effort to highlight more recent literature of China, we offer curriculum on two short stories. "Hands" (1936) by Xiao Hong tells the story of a young girl being bullied in school. It offers rich ground to explore the dynamics of bullying as well as class discrimination. Another exemplary story "Iron Child" (1992) by Nobel Prize winner Mo Yan shares a magical realistic tale of an orphan during the Great Leap Forward, a period of famine and social turmoil in China. These stories may resonate with students dealing with bullying and abandonment in altogether different contexts.

Both stories come from *The Columbia Anthology of Modern Chinese Literature* and, at the time of this book's publication, are available for free online through Google books. Other notable works of modern Chinese literature, also from *The Columbia Anthology of Modern Chinese Literature,* include:

- "Wrong Number" (1983) by Liu Yichang translated by Michael S. Duke, a short, short story about chance and death;
- "Dog" (1931) by Ba Jin translated by Lance Halvorsen, a story about a person who believes he is a dog;
- "The Steelyard" (1926) by Lai He translated by Howard Goldblatt, a short story about economic inequality and a corrupt criminal justice system.

For an immersive reading experience, we recommend *Rickshaw Boy* (1939) by Lao She translated by Howard Goldblatt. Told in language and a narrative style accessible to the average tenth grader, *Rickshaw Boy* (2010) by Lao She and translated by Howard Goldblatt shares the struggles of a poor country boy who moves to the big city with dreams of becoming wealthy. Despite talent and hard work, the main character encounters a number of setbacks that stymie his hopes. Thematically comparable to American classics such as *Of Mice and Men* or *The Great Gatsby*, *Rickshaw Boy* offers a powerful critique of class inequality and individualism worthy of reflection both in the context of Chinese history and in general. The ending of the *Rickshaw Boy* provides a cautionary tale relevant for anyone hailing from the east or west.

With these selections, many of which portray China as a poor country, we already run the risk of stereotyping. The stories here depict a China dominated by corrupt officials and crippled by poverty. The two short stories highlighted in this chapter similarly offer a bleak picture of China.

These translated stories are not written by outsiders with an unrealistic perception of China, however. They're not written by immigrants imagining the stories of their heritage countries. They are written by writers of China making social commentaries about the China they experienced firsthand. The pre-occupation with poverty, reflected in many of these selections, suggests the period of crisis that characterized pre-Communist China brought forth a number of dramatic stories worthy of remembering and better understanding.

"Iron Child" (1993) by Mo Yan (1955–) and Translated by Howard Goldblatt

Themes: Abandonment, Hunger
Topics: Orphans, Cannibalism, Industrialization/Trains

Key Terms

- Unreliable Narrator: a narrator whose view cannot be fully trusted because the narrator wants to hide something or doesn't fully understand what is happening.
- Dramatic Irony: the tension that emerges when the narrator does not understand what they are describing and the reader does.
- Magical Realism or Hallucinatory Realism: a fantastical style of storytelling that first emerged in Latin America, an unrealistic narrative style that reveals the deeper reality of a situation.

Mo Yan

Born to a farming family in 1955, the author Guan Moye dropped out of school in the fifth grade in the turmoil of the Cultural Revolution to do farm work and later work in a factory. In 1976, he joined the People's Liberation Army (PLA) where he began to write. During this time, he published numerous works under the pseudonym Mo Yan. His first novel *Red Sorghum* established his international reputation. The novel was adapted into a film and named best film at the Berlin Film Festival. Renowned for his magical realistic style, Mo Yan is regarded as one of China's foremost authors. He has been awarded several international prizes including the Nobel Prize in Literature in 2012. He has said that his work is influenced by William Faulkner, James Joyce, Gabriel Garcia Marquez, Mishima Yokio, and Oe Kenzaburo.

Howard Goldblatt

Having translated more than 50 books from Chinese into English, Goldblatt is the premier English language translator of much Chinese literature and prose. Born in Long Beach, California in 1939, Howard Goldblatt enlisted in the army after college. In 1962, Goldblatt was deployed to Taipei where he discovered Chinese culture and became a serious student of Chinese, a language whose cadence and humor he liked. While pursuing his dissertation back in the U.S. at Indiana University, Goldblatt came across the works and translated two novels of Xiao Hong who, by that time, had become relatively unknown even in China. Goldblatt discovered Mo Yan in 1988 when a friend sent him a copy of a Hong Kong literary magazine. Shortly after reading the story, Goldblatt wrote to the author and offered to be his English translator. Goldblatt served as a professor of Chinese Literature at San Francisco State University, the University of Colorado-Boulder, and Notre Dame, where he was director for the Center of Chinese Studies and where his wife Sylvia Lin also served also a professor.

Background

By 1993 when "Iron Child" was first published, China's experiment with communism was over, and Beijing already had its first McDonald's. The narrator of the story, however, takes the reader back to the Great Leap Forward (1958–1962) when the Communist Party under Chairman Mao Zedong attempted to transform China from an agrarian society to a modern industrial nation—in just five years. During this period, villages each maintained their own backyard steel furnace, intended to accelerate industrialization, and villages were encouraged to work as a commune. Without the heavy machinery or agricultural surplus that the Soviet Union enjoyed, however, the architects of the Great Leap Forward relied upon human labor instead of machinery to spur industrialization. Hurriedly and ineptly implemented with a series of natural disasters worsening the crisis, the Great Leap Forward is generally regarded as a cataclysmic failure; between 1959 and 1962, 20 million people in China died (Encyclopedia Brittanica, 2018).

The story is set during late 1950s and early 1960s during the period including the Great Leap Forward Movement and the famine that ensued. The villagers' work in building a railroad recalls the mass smelting campaigns during the Great Leap Forward Movement; the motifs of iron and hunger hence may also be seen as references to actual events.

The name of the main character, Gousheng, literally means "dog leftover." Although this name might be interpreted as a curse from his parents, in fact, some Chinese believe that giving children, especially boys, nonhuman, unattractive names—so bad that even dogs won't touch it—can prevent them from attracting the attention of the god of the underworld.

Summary

Told in a magical realistic style, *Iron Child* shares the story of Gousheng, a young boy abandoned by his parents and left at an orphanage at the age of three or four. Although the children do not engage in forced labor, their parents have been recruited to build a rail line. The orphanage feeds the children three bowls of porridge a day. And occasionally, a Caucasian man who works on the project taunts the children, telling them their parents have died. This man is later arrested.

As the project comes to an end, the children are told their parents will return. In celebration, the orphanage feeds the children fertilized egg, a strange treat, which the children are forced to eat. That day, the train passes through town, providing physical evidence that the project is complete.

With the orphanage closed, Gousheng must fend for himself. It is at this point in the story the magical realism begins in earnest. He meets Iron Child, a young boy like Gousheng. However, Iron Child is made of rusty iron. Iron Child and Gousheng walk toward and along the railroad tracks, and Iron Child shows Gousheng how to eat iron.

As they reach the end of the train tracks, Gousheng sees his mother and father eating dumplings and potatoes with eggs, but the smell of the food disgusts him. And Gousheng finds that his parents also disgust him. Iron Child helps Gousheng run away from his parents who continue to pursue him and lure him with food.

After successfully evading Gousheng's parents, some men in the area, including a man with a gimpy leg, call Gousheng and Iron Child "iron demons." The man with the gimpy leg points a pistol at the boys, but Iron Child snatches the pistol out of his hand. Iron Child and Gousheng eat part of the gun, but finding it tastes of gunpowder, toss it back to the gimpy man half-eaten.

That night, another train arrives into town crashing into the train already there, destroying the project.

For a time, Iron Child and Gousheng try to eat the newly smelted iron but do not find it as tasty as the rusty iron they prefer. The two are eventually captured and cleaned.

Discussion

Evading easy explanation, "Iron Child" presents a mysterious and thought-provoking story, raising a number of open-ended questions that make the story rich for classroom discussion. Who is Iron Child? What is the iron they are eating? Are all of Gousheng's experiences imagined or are some of his recollections true? Perhaps more importantly, why does Gousheng not want to go home to his parents? And why would Gousheng not want to eat real food? Though the story lends itself to a variety of interpretations, there is evidence to suggest that "Iron Child" can be read as a story about cannibalism.

Gousheng might be hallucinating that he is eating iron. His wild imagination makes sense given that hungry people will imagine anything in order to survive mentally.

There is also evidence to suggest Gousheng is partaking in actual cannibalism. As in *Life of Pi*, the character in the story creates an elaborate story in order to avoid the awful truth. The rusty iron, which Gousheng and Iron Child eat, might be dried blood, which in fact contains iron. The rusty "iron demons" might simply be two boys who have not bathed in months and are so filthy with soot, they no longer look human.

In the story, eating is consistently associated with something grotesque and dark. Rather than something happy and enjoyable, food is dark, eerie, and suspicious. We know that during the great famine, there were instances when people were so starved that they resorted to eating the dead, especially dead children. Combining this historical knowledge with our observation of the pattern in the story, we may draw a connection to the "stench" and this dark history.

When the project comes to an end, the orphanage feeds the children fertilized egg. Although considered a delicacy in some parts of the world, the narrator describes eating the feathers and beaks in some length, indicating he thinks it is strange. He describes the women at the orphanage smacking their lips hungrily as they eat it. These descriptions of eating half-formed feathers and beaks may be read as foreshadowing the cannibalism that occurs later in the story.

These explanations, however, do not shed light on why Gousheng would not want to go to his parents once he finds them. In answer to this question, students might point out that having been abandoned for so long and at such a young age, Gousheng may still harbor resentment toward his parents.

While some may suggest that Gousheng rejects his parents because he is angry with them for abandoning him, this interpretation does not explain Gousheng's behavior completely. Furthermore, this plausible reading of the story is not emphasized in the story. The story offers no evidence that he blames his parents for abandoning him or even that he feels abandoned. Rather the story suggests he feels liberated. This interpretation also fails to explain why his disgust centers on *food*.

Instead, the story suggests that Gousheng has undergone some sort of transformation as the result of eating iron. In Daoism, it is believed that once a person reaches a certain level of cultivation, s/he starts to draw sustenance from more ethereal sources than human food. Daoists believe that abstaining from human food allows a person to transcend the human condition. Similarly, we can say that since Gousheng has learned to eat something that is not human food, he too has taken leave of the human realm. An interesting question to ask: if Gousheng is no longer entirely human, what is he? Is he "above" the human realm like a transcendent Daoist, or is he "below," like a demon?

While students will not be able relate to the experience of cannibalism, the sensational nature of the topic is likely to draw a wide variety of students into the story. Students may relate the story of Gousheng's abandonment/liberation to their own experiences of getting lost and separated from their parents for an afternoon. Students might also relate Gousheng's experience to the disorientation and separation that can occur during and after a divorce or in adoption. These sensitive issues may be best shared in private journal writing activities or in small groups rather than in a large discussion.

Iron Child: Questions to Consider

1. Why were the children in an orphanage?
2. What happened to Gousheng after he left the orphanage?
3. Who was Iron Child? Do you think Iron Child is a figment of Gousheng's imagination or a real child? Provide evidence from the story to back up your reading.
4. Do you think Gousheng really eats iron?
5. What are some telltale signs that the story may not be entirely "realistic"? At what point do you notice?
6. What do you notice in the children's encounter with the sandy-haired young man? Why is he arrested? Do you think he is telling the truth or lying?
7. Find all the places where eating is described and note what happens in each instance. Can you see a pattern?
8. In the paragraph that describes the three women eating chicks, the narrator observes, "Their cheeks puffed out—first one side, then the other—and their lips smacked noisily. Tears flowed down from their eyes, which were shut the whole time" (382). Why are they crying?
9. Why does Gousheng reject his parents and find their food disgusting?

Iron Child: Activities

Close Reading Exercise: Find all the places in the story where eating is described and note what happens in each instance. Table 7.1 below provides an example.

The theme of the story maybe said to be hunger, but instead of telling a sad story full of suffering, the author playfully uses magical realism to transform hunger into a kind of superpower. The children are empowered by their ravenous appetite. But the traumatic reality does not disappear without leaving a mark on the story. We notice that whenever eating is mentioned, it is always accompanied by something dark or grotesque. Eating is denaturalized.

Table 7.1: Scene Analysis, "Iron Child."

Scene	**Analysis**
Children at the nursery are made to eat eggs with "feathery little chicks inside."	The image at once strikes the reader as grotesque. It is necessary, however, to pause for a moment to reflect on our own cultural biases when it comes to labeling other cultures' food "gross." In some cultures, eggs with unhatched chicks still inside are considered a delicacy. But these would be eggs that have failed to hatch, and eating them would be a way to prevent waste—an important value in traditional agrarian cultures. Of course, unlike the description in the story, the chicks would *not* be alive.
The three old women toss chicks into a pot of oil. Three "identical" old women are described as "skeletal" with "hawklike noses and sunken eyes," throwing chicks into a pot of foaming "light green" oil. "Their cheeks puffed out—first one side, then the other—and their lips smacked noisily. Tears flowed down from their eyes, which were shut the whole time."	The description here becomes increasingly surreal. We may ask: why? Is it because the scene is seen through the eyes of a hungry and scared child? Is he so hungry that he starts to hallucinate? The hallucinatory quality culminates in the image of three old women, evocative of witches. The first thing we notice is that the description about eating in this paragraph is full of sensory details, as if everything is enlarged and made more vivid by hunger. But why are the women crying? One possibility is that these are tears of remorse (the women don't want to eat the chicks, but they have no choice), but this interpretation is contradicted by the description of their lips ("smacked noisily"), which suggests enjoyment. The more likely interpretation then is that these are tears of joy. But this is no ordinary enjoyment. There is something primal or even obscene about this image of eating with excessive joy. This sense of weirdness is reinforced by what the child sees next (the sexually suggestive image of a snake eating a toad).

(Continued)

Table 7.1: (*Continued*)

Scene	**Analysis**
Gousheng runs into his parents. "What were they eating? Meaty dumplings and sweet potatoes with eggs. The food must be delicious, the way their cheeks were all puffed out, as if they had the mumps. But to me the stench of those meaty dumplings and sweet potatoes and eggs was worse than dog shit, and it made me so sick to my stomach I had to run downwind to avoid it."	They are eating, but Gousheng has a strange reaction to their re-union. Gousheng's reaction should strike us as odd. Why would a hungry child be repulsed by food, which, according to the narrator's own description, sounds delicious?

Source: Author.

Close Reading: Where Is Eating Described? What Happens in Each Scene?

Class Debate: If we accept that Gousheng engaged in cannibalism, was his cannibalism justified? Why or why not?

Journal Writing: Have you ever been abandoned by someone? What happened? How did you feel toward the person after the incident?

Research: After reading the story, as a class, compile questions students have about the Great Leap Forward. Using quality online sources, or other classroom or library resources, find answers to class questions and share these answers with the class.

"Hands" (1936) by Xiao Hong (1911–1942) and Translated by Howard Goldblatt

Themes: Bullying, Inequality, Discrimination
Topics: School, Life in a Dormitory

Key Terms

- Allusion: a reference to a literary work usually highlighting a key theme or similarity between the two texts.
- Dramatic Irony: the tension the emerges when the narrator does not understand what they are describing and the reader does.

Xiao Hong

Born in 1911 to a land-owning family in Northeast China, Xiao Hong ran away from home as a young adult in order to avoid an arranged marriage. Two years later, she met the writer Xiao Jun, with whom she led a bohemian and vagrant lifestyle. Hong rose to prominence with the publication of her first novel, *The Field of Life and Death* (1935), which recounted the difficulties of peasant life in the 1920s and 1930s particularly for women. In 1938, Xiao Hong and Xiao Jun separated and Hong married Duanmu Hongliang, another writer. In 1940, the two moved to Hong Kong where Hong finished *Tales of Hulan River*, a wryly humorous and semi-autobiographical work that depicted rural life and the rampant misogyny of the day. Shortly after the Japanese took over the British colony of Hong Kong, Hong died of respiratory problems. "Hands" has been called the artistically most accomplished of her short fiction.

Howard Goldblatt

Having translated more than 50 books from Chinese into English, Goldblatt is the premier English language translator of much Chinese literature and prose. Born in Long Beach, California in 1939, Howard Goldblatt enlisted in the army after college. In 1962, Goldblatt was deployed to Taipei where he discovered Chinese culture and became a serious student of Chinese, a language whose cadence and humor he liked. While pursuing his dissertation back in the U.S. at Indiana University, Goldblatt came across the works and translated two novels of Xiao Hong who, by that time, had become relatively unknown even in China. Goldblatt discovered Mo Yan in 1988 when a friend sent him a copy of a Hong Kong literary magazine. Shortly after reading the story, Goldblatt wrote to the author and offered to be his English translator. Goldblatt served as a professor of Chinese Literature at San Francisco State University, the University of Colorado-Boulder, and Notre Dame, where he was director for the Center of Chinese Studies and where his wife Sylvia Lin also served also a professor.

Background

Although the political context is not immediately relevant in the story, it may be important to note that the story was published in 1936 and predates China's industrialization and the rise of the Communist Party in China.

Like many nonwestern modernities, Chinese modernity originated in a traumatic encounter with Western imperialism. The project of modernizing China is therefore intrinsically paradoxical. Since the west set the standard for modernity, becoming modern means being more like the west, but adopting the western way of seeing the world means accepting or internalizing the west's racist views of the Chinese self. To be modern means to see oneself (from a racist point of view) as inferior.

Many modern Chinese writers have grappled with this paradox. Xiao Hong's story is unique in that it sets its sight on the seemingly progressive institution of modern education (and women's education at that). Unlike other modern Chinese writers who emphasize the conflict between tradition and modernity, Xiao Hong reveals that with its internalized racism and class prejudice, the idea of the modern can itself be oppressive and used to invalidate someone's lived experience and knowledge of the world.

Summary

The narrator introduces Wang Yaming, a girl with black and blue hands, known as "The Freak." Students laugh at Wang Yaming's English pronunciation when she stands for roll call. The teacher advises Wang to say "here" instead of "present," but Wang pronounces it "hayer," making the class roar with laughter.

Rather than go home at night or stay at the school's dormitory, every night, Wang Yaming hides in the bathroom where she studies. In the morning, she sits prominently at the foot of a staircase on campus. Despite Wang Yaming's poor performance in school, the narrator sees her studying hard even on a Sunday morning while everyone else is sleeping or getting ready to go out. The narrator speaks to Wang Yaming for the first time to wake her up one day.

Wang Yaming's father comes to visit Wang Yaming, and it becomes clear that Wang Yaming's family is poor; they cannot afford to buy Wang Yaming a pair of gloves. When the principal invites Wang Yaming's father to the reception room, he quickly departs because he believes he will be charged. As the father leaves, the narrator sees Wang Yaming's father's hands are also black.

The principal asks Wang Yaming to scrub the discoloration from her hands, because passersby can see her hands during morning calisthenics. As a result of her hands, Wang Yaming is not able to participate in these morning exercises, which everyone enjoys.

By spring, the narrator notices Wang Yaming is looking sickly and despondent, possibly because she is doing poorly in school and may be held back a year.

Later that spring, Wang Yaming, with her back toward her classmates, cries. The narrator notices that her hands appear to be lightening. The principal reprimands Wang Yaming for crying in front of visitors, for not maintaining her uniform, and for wearing gloves, which Wang Yaming wore to hide her dark hands. Despite the poor treatment, Wang Yaming returns the following year, her father dropping Wang Yaming off in a horsecart. Wang Yaming's hands are once again black.

In the dormitory, the other girls don't want to sleep next to Wang Yaming so Wang Yaming sleeps on a school bench. The principal directs Wang Yaming to take a place in the bed, which makes Wang Yaming happy. However, the housemother—who brags that she studied abroad in Japan—tells the girls that Wang Yaming is smelly and unsanitary. Despite the principal's best efforts, the girls at the dormitory refuse to sleep next to Wang Yaming. As a result, Wang Yaming returns to sleeping on the school bench in the corridor.

One day, Wang Yaming dyes her socks and blouses. Later, some girls find the eggs that they boiled are black, because, Wang Yaming admits, she used their pot for dyeing. Disgusted, the girls throw the pot and eggs to the ground. Wang Yaming salvages both.

The narrator says sometimes when no one else is around he walks alone with Wang Yaming in the bitter cold.

One morning, the narrator runs into Wang Yaming who can't get into a building because the custodian won't let her in. The narrator sits with Wang Yaming and reads a novel quietly. This is the first time he's been considerate to Wang Yaming, he realizes.

Hearing the narrator read aloud part of *The Jungle* by Upton Sinclair—a book about the injustices of the industrial revolution, Wang Yaming asks the narrator if she can borrow the book. When Wang Yaming returns with the book, she shares that she relates to one of the characters, Marija, because her family was also denied healthcare, a denial that led to her mother's death. She tells the narrator that her entire family work as dyers and that she is the only one able to go to school.

On her last day of school, Wang Yaming concentrates hard in her classes and takes note of everything, but the narrator finds that she has copied everything down incorrectly. After sleeping one last night on the bench, Wang Yaming's father comes to pick up Wang Yaming and Wang Yaming tells her father that she has been kicked out of school without taking her final exams. The narrator watches Wang Yaming and her father walk to the station to leave.

Discussion

The story of a young girl made fun of by her wealthier classmates, "Hands" shares a tragic story of bullying and raises questions about class and discrimination. Told from the point of view of a somewhat sympathetic classmate who grows closer to Wang Yaming as the story progresses, "Hands" is a story about wealth, color, and justice—themes relevant for many students today.

Immediately, the story pulls readers in with the central mystery: why are Wang Yaming's hands black? As the story progresses, the reader learns that Wang Yaming is desperately poor. An easy target, Wang Yaming, nevertheless has spunk and is not afraid to say what she thinks.

The story raises questions on the nature of bullying and the role of teachers in addressing bullying. Why do people pick on the weak and vulnerable? What is the role of bystanders in such a situation? The teachers in the story are complicit in the bullying, begging the question: what is the responsibility of teachers and school officials when children are made fun of? Given that bullying can have long-lasting consequences on an individual's development and identity formation, what can and should adults do?

Despite the narrator's close observations of Wang Yaming, he or she remains detached and never comes to Wang Yaming's aid or defense. The narrator talks to Wang Yaming, suggesting the two are friends; the narrator socializes with Wang Yaming and doesn't seem to care what others think despite Wang Yaming's lowly status at the school. Yet there is also evidence to suggest the narrator notices and judges Wang Yaming for her uncleanliness and her poor performance in school. How can readers reconcile these two readings?

The story should provoke reflection on readers' own experience of being made fun of or of making fun of others. What are students' stories of bullying? What are the lessons they learned from their experiences? How does it compare to Wang Yaming's experience? Personal reflection and sharing of student stories online or in person may be worthy of a full day to supplement reading and discussion of the text.

Hands: Discussion Questions

1. Why do students make fun of Wang Yaming? What are the two things that make Wang Yaming stand out in our first impression of her?
2. What is the reason for Wang Yaming's black hands?
3. Do the other students treat Wang Yaming unfairly? When and why do classmates treat her unfairly? Do the teachers and

principals treat her unfairly? When and why do they treat her unfairly?

4. The narrator and Wang Yaming both read *The Jungle*, a book that sheds light on the injustices of the industrial revolution. Researching online, find out more about *The Jungle*. Why do you think Wang Yaming is so moved by this book? What are the similarities between this book and Wang Yaming's story in "Hands."
5. Are Wang Yaming and the narrator friends? What details from the story suggest they are (or are not) friends?
6. Why did the principal kick Wang Yaming out of school without giving her the chance to take her final exam? Was this expulsion fair?
7. Do you think Wang Yaming was dumb? What evidence does the story offer to suggest that Wang Yaming is dumb or not dumb?
8. What sort of knowledge is privileged in this story? What sort of knowledge is ignored or not considered valuable?
9. How is the story organized? How many episodes are there? Can you observe any sort of progression?
10. Why is English so important in the story? What do you think English stands for?
11. Locate all the places where hands are mentioned. Can you identify a pattern?
12. How would you describe the narrator's relationship with Wang Yaming? Are they friends? What details from the story suggest that they are or are not? Do you notice any change in the relationship? What is the significance?
13. Why do you think the narrator's gender is not given?
14. Can you think of situations similar to Wang Yaming's in your own life?

Hands: Activities

Close Reading: Locate all the places where hands are mentioned. In each instance, what are hands associated with? Do you see a pattern? Table 7.2 provides ideas to get started.

Wang Yaming is singled out, mocked, and discriminated against because of her hands, which mark her as different from others in the school. In the story, hands have the following associations: (1) class status and manual labor; (2) hygiene and contamination; (3) skin tone.

Table 7.2: Scene Analysis, "Hands."

Scene	**Association**	**Analysis**
	Class status/ Manual labor	Wang's classmates' and teachers' scorn for her hands shows their contempt for manual labor. This tells us that the educational goal of the school is not to offer knowledge to a laborer's daughter but to prepare young women for a comfortable middle-class life.
	Hygiene and contamination	The importance of hygiene is particularly important in this historical period when hygiene was considered a necessary component of modernization and nation-building.
"'During morning calisthenics out on the playground there are several hundred white hands up in the air—all but yours; no, yours are special, very special!"	Skin tone	The principal exalts in the need for uniformity. Why is uniformity so important? As she explains, "Our school wall is low, and there are a lot of foreigners strolling by on spring days to take a look." Does this marked contrast between the principal's and other students' whiteness and Wang Yaming's blackened hands add a racial dimension to the discrimination based on hands? There is some evidence to support this interpretation. The principal's concern for how black hands would look reveals a certain assumption about what it means to be modern and to have knowledge. According to this assumption, held by most in this school, one can only be modern and have knowledge if one fits into the mold of a middle-class, westernized subject.

(Continued)

Table 7.2: *(Continued)*

Scene	Association	Analysis
"With her lips opening and closing, the principal reached out with her pale white fingers and clutched at Wang Yaming's collar …"	Skin tone	

Source: Author.

Close Reading: Where Are Hands Mentioned? What Are They Associated with?

Silent discussion: Through online or hard copy notes, which students can pass to one another in class, have students write down a story of bullying they witnessed or were a part of. Students can read and/or respond to one another through writing in class. Following small group or online sharing, the class can regroup to discuss the lessons learned from their shared experiences.

Dramatization: Using props and costumes, students can dramatize one of the following scenes from the story:

- The girls don't want to sleep next to Wang Yaming.
- The father visits Wang Yaming at school.
- Wang Yaming cries. The principal reprimands her for crying, for having a dirty uniform, and for wearing gloves.
- The narrator and Wang Yaming talk after Wang Yaming has read *The Jungle*.

Story Map: List the Main Events in the Story. Do You Notice a Progression?

Story Map: "Hands" is told in three sections or approximately fourteen scenes. Creating an Excel spreadsheet or a hand drawing, make a map of the story. Table 7.3 provides an example to get started. List all the sections or scenes and summarize the main event featured in each. Do you notice any movement or progression from episode to episode?

Table 7.3: Scene Analysis Continued, "Hands."

Scene	**Tormenter**	**Injury**	**Wang's physical & mental condition**	**Relationship to Narrator**
School	Principal		Wang is confident and upbeat.	Narrator is suspicious of Wang Yaming.
Summer Break	Fellow students	Wang is forced to sleep in corridor		
		Wang is not allowed to finish her final exams.		Narrator is sympathetic to Wang Yaming.

Source: Author.

Hands[1]
By Xiao Hong (1911–1942)
Translated by Howard Goldblatt

Never had any of us in the school seen hands the likes of hers before: blue, black, and even showing a touch of purple, the discoloring ran from her fingertips all the way to her wrists.

We called her "The Freak" the first few days she was here. After class we always crowded around her, but not one of us had ever asked her about her hands.

Try though we might, when our teacher took roll call, we just could not keep from bursting out laughing:

"Li Jie!" "Present."

"Zhang Zhufang!" "Present."

"Xu Guizhen!" "Present."

One after another in rapid, orderly fashion, we stood up as our names were called, then sat back down. But when it came Wang Yaming's turn, the process lengthened considerably.

"Hey, Wang Yaming! She's calling your name!" One of us often had to prod her before she finally stood up, her blackened hands hanging stiffly at her sides, her shoulders drooping. Staring at the ceiling, she would answer: "Pre-se-nt!"

No matter how the rest of us laughed at her, she would never lose her composure but merely push her chair back noisily with a solemn air and sit down after what seemed like several moments. Once, at the beginning of English class, our English teacher was laughing so hard she had to remove her glasses and wipe her eyes.

"Next time you need not answer *hay-er,*" she commented. "Just say 'present' in Chinese."

We were all laughing and scuffling our feet on the floor. But on the following day in English class, when Wang Yaming's name was called we were once again treated to sounds of "*Hay-er, hay-er*."

"Have you ever studied English before?" the English teacher asked as she adjusted her glasses slightly.

"You mean the language they speak in England? Sure, I've studied some, from the pockmarked teacher. Let's see, I know that they write with a *pun-sell* or a *pun,* but I never heard *hay-er* before."

"'Here' simply means 'present.' It's pronounced 'here,' 'h-e-r-e.'"

"*She-er, she-er.*" And so she began saying *she-er.* Her quaint pronunciation made everyone in the room laugh so hard we literally shook. All, that is, except Wang Yaming, who sat down very calmly and opened her book with her blackened hands. Then she began reading in a very soft voice: "*Who-at … deez … ahar …*"[2]

During math class she read her formulas the same way she read essays: "$2x + y = \ldots x\ 2 = \ldots$"

At the lunch table, as she reached out to grab a *mantou*[3] with a blackened hand, she was still occupied with her geography lesson: "Mexico produces silver … Yunnan … hmm, Yunnan produces marble."

At night she hid herself in the bathroom and studied her lessons, and at the crack of dawn she could be found sitting at the foot of the stairs. Wherever there was the slightest glimmer of light, that's where I usually found her. One morning during a heavy snowfall, when the trees outside the window were covered with a velvety layer of white, I thought I spotted someone sleeping on the ledge of the window at the far end of the corridor in our dormitory.

"Who's there? It's so cold there!" The slapping of my shoes on the wooden floor produced a hollow sound. Since it was a Sunday morning, there was a pronounced stillness throughout the school; some of the girls were getting ready to go out, while others were still in bed asleep. Even before I had drawn up next to her I noticed the pages of the open book on her lap turning over in the wind. "Who do we have here? How can anybody be studying so hard on a Sunday!" Just as I was about to wake the girl up a pair of blackened hands suddenly caught my eye. "Wang Yaming! Hey, come on, wake up now!" This was the first time I had ever called her name, and it gave me a strange, awkward feeling.

"*Haw-haw* … I must have fallen asleep!"

Every time she spoke she prefaced her remarks with a dull-witted laugh. "*Who-at … deez … yoou … ai,*" she began to read before she had even found her place in the book.

"*Who-at … deez …* this English is sure hard. It's nothing like our Chinese characters with radicals and the like. No, all it has is a lot of squiggles, like a bunch of worms crawling around in my brain, getting me more confused all the time, until I can't remember any more. Our English teacher says it isn't hard—not hard, she says. Well, maybe not for the rest of you. But me, I'm stupid; we country folk just aren't as quick-witted as the rest of you. And my father's even worse off than me. He said that when he was young he only learned one character—our name Wang—and he couldn't even remember that one for more than a few minutes. *Yoou ... ai ... yoou ... ah-ar ...*" Finishing what she had to say, she tacked on a series of unrelated words from her lesson.

The ventilator on the wall whirred in the wind, as snowflakes were blown in through the window, where they stuck and turned into beads of ice. Her eyes were all bloodshot; like her blackened hands, they were greedily striving for a goal that was forever just beyond reach. In the corners of rooms or any place where even a glimmer of light remained, we saw her, looking very much like a mouse gnawing away at something.

The first time her father came to visit her he said she had gained weight: "I'll be damned, you've put on a few pounds. The chow here must be better'n it is at home, ain't that right? You keep working hard! You study here for three years or so, and even though you won't turn into no sage, at least you'll know a little somethin' about the world."

For a solid week after his visit we had a great time mimicking him. The second time he came she asked him for a pair of gloves.

"Here, you can have this pair of mine! Since you're studyin' your lessons so hard, you oughta at least have a pair of gloves. Here, don't you worry none about it. If you want some gloves, then go ahead and wear these. It's comin' on spring now, and I don't go out much anyway. Little Ming, we'll just buy another pair next winter, won't we, Little Ming?" He was standing in the doorway of the reception room bellowing, and a crowd of his daughter's classmates had gathered around him. He continued calling out "Little Ming this" and "Little Ming that," then gave her some news from home: "Third Sister went visitin' over to Second Auntie's and stayed for two or three days! Our little pig has been gettin' a couple extra handfuls of beans every day, and he's so fat now you've never seen the like. His ears are standin' straight up. Your elder sister came home and pickled two more jars of scallions."

He was talking so much he had worked up a sweat, and just then the school principal threaded her way through the crowd of onlookers and walked up to him: "Won't you please come into the reception room and have a seat?"

"No thanks, there's no need for that, that'll just waste everyone's time. Be- sides, I couldn't if I wanted to; I have to go catch a train back home. All those kids at home, I don't feel right leavin' 'em there." He took his cap off and held it in his hands, then he nodded to the principal. Steam rose from his head as he pushed the door open and strode out, looking as though he had been chased off by the principal. But he stopped in his tracks and turned around, then began removing his gloves.

"Daddy, you keep them. I don't need to wear gloves anyway."

Her father's hands were also discolored, but they were both bigger and blacker than Wang Yaming's.

Later, when we were in the reading room, Wang Yaming asked me: "Tell me, is it true? If someone goes into the reception room to sit and chat, does it cost them anything?"

"Cost anything! For what?"

"Not so loud; if the others hear you, they'll start laughing at me again." She placed the palm of her hand on top of the newspaper I was reading and continued: "My father said so. He said there was a teapot and some cups in the reception room, and that if he went inside the custodian would probably pour tea, and that he would have to pay for it. I said he wasn't expected to, but he wouldn't believe me, and he said that even in a small teahouse, if you went in and just had a cup of water you'd have to pay something. It was even more likely in a school; he said, 'Just think how big a school is!'"

The principal said to her, as she had several times in the past: "Can't you wash those hands of yours clean? Use a little more soap! Wash them good and hard with hot water. During morning calisthenics out on the playground there are several hundred white hands up in the air—all but yours; no, yours are special, very special!" The principal reached out her bloodless, fossil-like transparent fingers and touched Wang Yaming's blackened hands. Holding her breath somewhat fearfully, she looked as though she were reaching out to pick up a dead crow. "They're a lot less stained than they used to be—I can even see the skin on the palms now. They're much better than they were when you first got here—they were like hands of iron then! Are you keeping up with your lessons? I want you to work a little harder, and from now on you don't have to take part in morning calisthenics. Our school wall is low, and there are a lot of foreigners strolling by on spring days who stop to take a look. You can join in again when the discoloring on your hands is all gone!" This lecture by the school principal was to bring an end to her morning calisthenics.

"I already asked my father for a pair of gloves. No one would notice them if I had gloves on, would they?" She opened up her book bag and took out the gloves her father had given her.

The principal laughed so hard at this she fell into a fit of coughing. Her pallid face suddenly reddened. "What possible good would that do? What we want is uniformity, and even if you wore gloves you still wouldn't be like the others."

The snow atop the artificial hill had melted, the bell being rung by the school custodian produced a crisper sound than usual, sprouts began to appear on the willow trees in front of the window, and a layer of steam rose from the playground under the rays of the sun. As morning calisthenics began, the sound of the exercise leader's whistle carried far into the distance; its echo reverberated among the people in the clump of trees outside the windows. We ran and jumped like a flock of noisy birds, intoxicated by the sweet fragrance that drifted over from the new buds on the branches of the trees. Our spirits, which had been imprisoned by the winter weather, were set free anew, like cotton wadding that has just been released.

As the morning calisthenics period was coming to an end we suddenly heard someone calling to us from an upstairs window in a voice that seemed to be floating up to the sky: "Just feel how warm the sun is! Aren't you hot down there? Aren't you ..."

There standing in the window behind the budding willows was Wang Yaming.

By the time the trees were covered with green leaves and were casting their shade all over the compound, a change had come over Wang Yaming—she had begun to languish and black circles had appeared around her eyes. Her ears seemed less full than before and her strong shoulders began to slump. On one of the rare occasions when I saw her under one of the shade trees I noticed her slightly hollow chest and was reminded of someone suffering from consumption.

"The principal says my schoolwork's lagging behind, and she's right, of course; if it hasn't improved by the end of the year, well … *Haw-haw!* Do you think she'll really keep me back a year?" Even though her speech was still punctuated with that *haw-haw,* I could see that she was trying to hide her hands—she kept the left one behind her back, while all I could see of the right one was a lump under the sleeve of her jacket.

We had never seen her cry before, but one gusty day when the branches of the trees outside the windows were bending in the wind, she stood there with her back to the classroom and to the rest of us and wept to the wind outside. This occurred after a group of visitors had departed, and she stood there wiping the tears from her eyes with darkened hands that had already lost a good deal of their color.

"Are you crying? How dare you cry! Why didn't you go away and hide when all the visitors were here? Just look at yourself. You're the only 'special case' in the whole group! Even if I were to forget for the moment those two blue hands of yours, just look at your uniform—it's almost gray! Everybody else has on a blue blouse, but you, you're special. It doesn't look good to have someone wearing clothes so old that the color has faded. We can't let our system of uniforms go out the window because of you alone." With her lips opening and closing, the principal reached out with her pale white fingers and clutched at Wang Yaming's collar. "I told you to go downstairs and not come back up until after the visitors had left! Who told you to stand out there in the corridor? Did you really think they wouldn't see you out there? And to top it all, you had on this pair of oversized gloves."

As she mentioned the word *gloves* the principal kicked the glove that had dropped to the floor with the shiny toe of her patent shoe and said: "I suppose you figured everything would be just fine if you stood out there wearing a pair of gloves, didn't you? What kind of nonsense is that?" She kicked the glove again, but this time, looking at that huge glove, which was large enough for a carter to wear, she couldn't suppress a chuckle.

How Wang Yaming cried that time; she was still weeping even after the sounds of the wind had died down.

She returned to the school after summer vacation. The late summer weather was as cool and brisk as autumn, and the setting sun turned the cobbled road a deep red. We had gathered beneath the crab-apple tree by the school entrance and were eating crab-apples when a horsecart from Mount Lama carrying Wang Yaming rumbled up. In the silence following the arrival of the cart her father began taking her luggage down for her, while she held on to her small washbasin and a few odds and ends. We didn't immediately make way for her when she reached the step of the gate. Some of us called out to her: "So here you are! You've come back!" Others just stood there gaping at her. As her father followed her up to the steps, the white towel which hung from his waistband flapping to and fro, someone said: "What's this? After spending a summer at home, her hands are as black as they were before. Don't they look like they're made of iron?"

I didn't really pay much attention to her ironlike hands until our post- autumn moving day. Although I was half asleep, I could hear some quarreling in the next room:

"I don't want her. I won't have my bed next to hers!" "I don't want mine next to hers either."

I tried listening more attentively, but I couldn't hear clearly what was going on. All I could hear was some muffled laughter and an occasional sound of commotion. But going out into the corridor that night to get a drink of water, I saw someone sleeping on one of the benches. I recognized her at once—it was Wang Yaming. Her face was covered with those two blackened hands, and her quilt had slid down so that half was on the ground and the other half barely covered her legs. I thought that she was getting in some studying by the corridor light, but I saw no books beside her. There was only a clutter of personal belongings and odds and ends on the floor all around her.

On the next day the principal, followed closely by Wang Yaming, made her way among the neatly arranged beds, snorting as she did so and testing the freshly tucked bedsheets with her delicate fingers.

"Why, here's a row of seven beds with only eight girls sleeping on them; some of the others have nine girls sleeping in six beds!" As she said this she took one of the quilts and moved it slightly to one side, telling Wang Yaming to place her bedding there.

Wang Yaming opened up her bedding and whistled contentedly as she made up the bed. This was the first time I had ever heard anyone whistle in school. After she made up the bed she sat on it, her mouth open and her chin tilted slightly higher than usual, as though she were calmed by a feeling of repose and a sense of contentment. The principal had already turned and gone downstairs, and was perhaps by then out of the dormitory altogether and on her way home. But the old housemother with lackluster hair kept shuffling back and forth, scraping her shoes on the floor.

"As far as I'm concerned," she said, "this won't do at all. It's unsanitary. Who wants to be with her, with those vermin all over her body?" As she took a few steps toward the corner of the room, she seemed to be staring straight at me. "Take a look at that bedding! Have a sniff at it! You can smell the odor two feet away. Just imagine how ludicrous it is to have to sleep next to her! Who knows, those vermin of hers might hop all over anyone next to her. Look at this, have you ever seen cotton wadding as filthy as that?"

The housemother often told us stories about how she had accompanied her husband overseas to study in Japan, and how she should be considered an overseas student also. When asked by some of the girls: "What did you study?" she would respond: "Why study any particular subject? I picked up some Japanese and noticed some Japanese customs while I was there. Isn't that studying abroad?" Her speech was forever dotted with terms like "unsanitary," "ludicrous," "filthy," and so on, and she always called lice "vermin."

"If someone's filthy the hands show it." When she said the word *filthy* she shrugged her broad shoulders, as though she had been struck by a blast of cold air, then suddenly darted outside.

"This kind of student! Really, the principal shouldn't have …" Even after the lights-out bell had sounded the housemother could still be heard talking with some of the girls in the corridor.

On the third night Wang Yaming, bundle in hand and carrying her bedding, was again walking along behind the white-faced principal.

"We don't want her. We already have enough girls here."

They started yelling before the principal had even laid a finger on their bedding, and the same thing happened when she moved on to the next row of beds.

"We're too crowded here already! Do you expect us to take any more? Nine girls on six beds; how are we supposed to take any more?"

"One, two, three, four …" the principal counted. "Not enough; you can still add one more. There should be six girls for every four beds, but you only have five. Come on over here, Wang Yaming!"

"No, my sister's coming tomorrow, and we're saving that space for her," one of the girls said as she ran over and held her bedding in place.

Eventually the principal led her over to another dormitory. "She's got lice. I'm not going to sleep next to her."

"I'm not going to either."

"Wang Yaming's bedding doesn't have a cover and she sleeps right next to the cotton wadding. If you don't believe me, just look for yourself!"

Then they began to joke about it, saying they were all afraid of Wang Yaming's black hands and didn't dare get close to her.

Finally the black-handed girl had to sleep on a bench in the corridor. On mornings when I got up early I met her there rolling up her bedding and carrying it downstairs. Sometimes I ran into her in the basement storage room. Naturally, that was always at nighttime, so when we talked I kept looking at the shadows cast on the wall; the shadows of her hands as she scratched her head were the same color as her black hair.

"Once you get used to it, you can sleep on a bench or even on the floor. After all, sleep is sleep no matter where you lie down, so what's the difference? Studying is what matters. I wonder what sort of grade Mrs. Ma is going to give me in English on our next exam. If I don't score at least sixty I'll be kept back at the end of the year, won't I?"

"Don't worry about that; they won't keep you back just because of one subject," I assured her.

"But Daddy told me I only have three years to graduate in. He said he won't be able to handle the tuition for even one extra semester. But this English language—I just can't get my tongue right for it. *Haw-haw* …"

Everyone in the dormitory was disgusted with her, even though she was sleeping in the corridor, because she was always coughing during the night. Another reason was that she had begun to dye her socks and blouses right in the dormitory.

"When clothes get old, if you dye them they're as good as new. Like, if you take a summer uniform and dye it gray, then you can use it as an autumn uniform. You can dye a pair of white socks black, then …"

"Why don't you just buy a pair of black socks?" I asked her.

"You mean those sold in the stores? When they dye them they use too much alum, so not only don't they hold up, but they tear as soon as you put them on. It's a lot better to dye them yourself. Socks are so expensive it just won't do to throw them away as soon as they have holes in them."

One Saturday night some of the girls cooked some eggs in a small iron pot, something they did nearly every Saturday, as they wanted to have something special to eat. I saw the eggs they cooked this time when they took them out of the pot. They were black, looking to me as if they had been poisoned or some- thing. The girl who carried the eggs in roared so loudly her glasses nearly fell off: "All right, who did it! Who? Who did this!?"

Wang Yaming looked over at the girl as she squeezed her way through the others into the kitchen. After a few *haw-haw*'s she said: "It was me. I didn't know anyone was going to use this pot, so I dyed two pairs of socks in it. *Haw- haw* … I'll go and …"

"You'll go and do what?"

"I'll go and wash it."

"You think we'd cook eggs in the same pot you used to dye your stinky old socks! Who wants it?" The iron pot was hurled to the floor, where it clanged in front of us. Scowling, the girl wearing glasses then flung the blackened eggs to the floor as though she were throwing stones.

After everyone else had left the scene, Wang Yaming picked the eggs up off the floor, saying to herself: "Hm! Why throw a perfectly good iron pot away just because I dyed a couple of pairs of socks in it? Besides, how could new socks be 'stinky'?"

On snowy winter nights the path from the school to our dormitories was completely covered by a blanket of snow. We just pushed on ahead as best we could, bumping our way along, and when we ran into a strong wind we either turned around and walked backward or walked sideways against the wind and snow. In the mornings we had to set out again from our dormitories, and in December it got so bad that our feet were numb with the cold, even if we ran. All of this caused a lot of grumbling and complaining, and some of the girls even began calling the principal names for placing the dormitories so far from the school and for making us leave for school before dawn.

Sometimes I met Wang Yaming as I was walking alone. There would be a sparkle to the sky and the distant snow cover as we walked along together, the moon casting our shadows ahead of us. There would be no other people in sight as the wind whistled through the trees by the side of the road and windows creaked and groaned under the driving snow. Our voices had harsh sounds to them as we talked in the sub-zero weather until our lips turned as stiff and numb as our legs and we stopped talking altogether, at which time we could hear only the crunching of the snow beneath our feet. When we rang the bell at the gate our legs were so cold they felt like they were about to fall off, and our knees were about to buckle under us.

One morning—I forget just when it was—I walked out of the dormitory with a novel I wanted to read tucked under my arm, then turned around and pulled the door shut tight behind me. I felt very ill at ease as I looked at the blurred houses off in the distance and heard the sound of the shifting snow behind me; I grew more frightened with every step. The stars gave off only a glimmer of light, and the moon either had already set or was covered by the gray, dirty- looking clouds in the sky. Every step I took seemed to add another step to the distance I had yet to go. I hoped I would meet someone along the way, but dreaded it at the same time; for on a moonless night you could hear the footsteps long before you saw anyone, until the figure suddenly appeared without warning right in front of you.

When I reached the stone steps of the school gate my heart was pounding, and I rang the door bell with a trembling hand. Just then I heard someone on the steps behind me.

"Who is it? Who's there?"

"Me! It's me."

"Were you walking behind me all the time?" It gave me quite a fright, because I hadn't heard any steps but my own on the way over.

"No, I wasn't walking behind you; I've already been here a long time. The custodian won't open the door for me. I don't know how long I've been here shouting for him."

"Didn't you ring the bell?"

"It didn't do any good, *haw-haw*. The custodian turned on the light and came to the door, then he looked out through the window. But he wouldn't open the door for me."

The light inside came on and the door opened noisily, accompanied by some angry scolding: "What's the idea of shouting at the gate at all hours of the night? You're going to wind up at the bottom of the class anyway, so why worry about it?"

"What's going on! What's that you're saying?" Before I had even finished, the custodian's manner changed completely.

"Oh, Miss Xiao, have you been waiting there long?"

Wang Yaming and I walked to the basement together; she was coughing and her face, which had grown pale and wrinkled, shivered for a few moments. With tears induced by the cold wind on her cheeks, she sat down and opened her school book.

"Why wouldn't the custodian open the door for you?" I asked.

"Who knows? He said I was too early. He told me to go on back, saying that he was only following the principal's orders."

"How long were you waiting out there?"

"Not too long. Only a short while … a short while. I guess about as long as it takes to eat a meal. *Haw-haw*."

She no longer studied her lessons as she had when she first arrived. Her voice was much softer now and she just muttered to herself. Her swaying shoulders slumped forward and were much narrower than they had been, while her back was no longer straight and her chest had grown hollow. I read my novel, but very softly so as not to disturb her. This was the first time I had been so considerate, and I wondered why it was only the first time. She asked me what novels I had read and whether I knew *The Romance of the Three Kingdoms*. Every once in a while she picked the book up and looked at its cover or flipped through the pages. "You and the others are so smart. You don't even have to look at your lessons and you're still not the least bit worried about exams. But not me. Sometimes I feel like taking a break and reading something else for a change, but that just doesn't work with me."

One Sunday, when the dormitory was deserted, I was reading aloud the passage in Sinclair's *The Jungle* where the young girl laborer Marija had collapsed in the snow. I gazed out at the snow-covered ground outside the window and was moved by the scene. Wang Yaming was standing right behind me, though I was unaware of it.

"Would you lend me one of the books you've already read? This snowy weather depresses me. I don't have any family around here, and there's nothing to shop for out on the street—besides, everything costs money."

"Your father hasn't been to see you for a long time, has he?" I thought she might be feeling a little homesick.

"How could he come? A round trip on the train costs two dollars, and then there'd be nobody at home."

I handed her my copy of *The Jungle,* since I had read it before.

She laughed—"*haw-haw*"—then patted the edge of the bed a couple of times and began examining the cover of the book. After she walked out of the room, I could hear her in the corridor reading the first sentence of the book loudly just as I had been doing.

One day sometime after that—again I forget just when it was, but it must have been another holiday—the dormitory was deserted all day long, right up to the time that moonlight streamed in through the windows, and the whole place was extremely lonely. I heard a rustling sound from the end of the bed, as though someone were there groping around for something. Raising my head to take a look, I noticed Wang Yaming's blackened hands in the moonlight. She was placing the book she had borrowed beside me.

"Did you like it?" I asked her. "How was it?"

At first she didn't answer me; then, covering her face with her hands and trembling, she said: "Fine."

Her voice was quivering. I sat up in bed, but she moved away, her face still buried in hands as black as the hair on her head. The long corridor was completely deserted, and my eyes were fixed on the cracks in the wooden floor, which were illuminated by moonlight.

"Marija is a very real person to me. You don't think she died after she collapsed in the snow, do you? She couldn't have died. Could she? The doctor knew she didn't have any money, though, so he wouldn't treat her … *haw- haw*." Her high-pitched laugh brought tears to her eyes. "I went for a doctor once myself, when my mother was sick, but do you think he would come? First he wanted travel money, but I told him all our money was at home. I begged him to come with me then, because she was in a bad way. Do you think he would agree to come with me? He just stood there in the courtyard and asked me: 'What does your family do? You're dyers, aren't you?' I don't know why, but as soon as I told him we were dyers he turned and walked back inside. I waited for a while, but he didn't come back out, so I knocked on his door again. He said to me through the door: 'I won't be able to take care of your mother, now just go away!' so I went back home." She wiped her eyes again, then continued:

"From then on I had to take care of my two younger brothers and two younger sisters. Daddy used to dye the black and blue things, and my elder sister dyed the red ones. Then in the winter of the year that my elder sister was engaged her future mother-in-law came in from the countryside to stay with us. The moment she saw my elder sister she cried out: 'My God, those are the hands of a murderess!' After that, Daddy no longer let anyone dye only red things or only blue things. My hands are black, but if you look closely you can see traces of purple; my two younger sisters' hands are the same."

"Aren't your younger sisters in school?"

"No. Later on I'll teach them their lessons. Except that I don't know how well I'm doing myself, and if I don't do well then I won't even be able to face my younger sisters. The most we can earn for dyeing a bolt of cloth is thirty cents. How many bolts do you think we get a month? One article of clothing is a dime—big or small—and nearly everyone sends us overcoats. Take away the cost for fuel and for the dyes, and you can see what I mean. In order to pay my tuition they had to save every penny, even going without salt, so how could I even think of not doing my lessons? How could I?" She reached out and touched the book again.

My gaze was still fixed on the cracks in the floor, thinking to myself that her tears were much nobler than my sympathy.

One morning just before our winter holiday Wang Yaming was occupied with putting her personal belongings in order. Her luggage was already firmly bound, standing at the base of the wall. Not a soul went over to say good-bye to her. As we walked out of the dormitory, one by one, and passed by the bench that had served as Wang Yaming's bed, she smiled at each of us, at the same time casting glances through the window off into the distance. We shuffled along down the corridor, then walked downstairs and across the courtyard. As we reached the gate at the fence, Wang Yaming caught up with us, panting hard through her widely opened mouth.

"Since my father hasn't come yet, I might as well get in another hour's class work. Every hour counts," she announced to everyone present.

She worked up quite a sweat in this final hour of hers. She copied down every single word from the blackboard during the English class into a little notebook. She read them aloud as she did so and even copied down words she already knew as the teacher casually wrote them on the board. During the following hour, in geography class, she very laboriously copied down the maps the teacher had drawn on the board. She acted as though everything that went through her mind on this her final day had taken on great importance, and she was determined to let none of it pass unrecorded.

When class let out I took a look at her notebook, only to discover that she had copied it all down incorrectly. Her English words had either too few or too many letters. She obviously had a very troubled heart.

Her father still hadn't come to fetch her by nightfall, so she spread her bedding out once again on the bench. She had never before gone to bed as early as she did that night, and she slept much more peacefully than usual. Her hair was spread out over the quilt, her shoulders were relaxed, and she breathed deeply; there were no books beside her that night.

Notes

1. Story reprinted here with permission from Columbia University Press.
2. "What ... these ... are ..."
3. Chinese steamed bread.

Reference

Great Leap Forward. Encyclopedia Brittanica. https://www.britannica.com/event/Great-Leap-Forward.

Contributor Biography

Yun Peng is Associate Professor in the Department of East Asian Languages and Literatures at the University of Hawai'i at Manoa. She received a Ph.D. in comparative literature from the University of Minnesota. Her research interests include modern Chinese literature, Chinese cinema, literary criticism, and film theory. Her current work focuses on contemporary Chinese documentary and independent films.

Index

G

H

I

K

L

M

P

S

U

W

Y

Z

www.ingramcontent.com/pod-product-compliance
Ingram Content Group UK Ltd.
Pitfield, Milton Keynes, MK11 3LW, UK
UKHW021010120926
8556IPUK00029B/443

9 781433 164163